From Xerxes' Murder (465) to Arridaios' Execution (317)

Updates to Achaemenid chronology
(including errata in past reports)

Leo Depuydt

BAR International Series 1887
2008

Published in 2016 by
BAR Publishing, Oxford

BAR International Series 1887

From Xerxes' Murder (465) to Arridaios' Execution (317)

ISBN 978 1 4073 0367 3

© L Depuydt and the Publisher 2008

The author's moral rights under the 1988 UK Copyright,
Designs and Patents Act are hereby expressly asserted.

All rights reserved. No part of this work may be copied, reproduced, stored,
sold, distributed, scanned, saved in any form of digital format or transmitted
in any form digitally, without the written permission of the Publisher.

BAR Publishing is the trading name of British Archaeological Reports (Oxford) Ltd.
British Archaeological Reports was first incorporated in 1974 to publish the BAR
Series, International and British. In 1992 Hadrian Books Ltd became part of the BAR
group. This volume was originally published by Archaeopress in conjunction with
British Archaeological Reports (Oxford) Ltd / Hadrian Books Ltd, the Series principal
publisher, in 2008. This present volume is published by BAR Publishing, 2016.

Printed in England

BAR titles are available from:

	BAR Publishing
	122 Banbury Rd, Oxford, OX2 7BP, UK
EMAIL	info@barpublishing.com
PHONE	+44 (0)1865 310431
FAX	+44 (0)1865 316916
	www.barpublishing.com

This investigation consists of updates to the chronology of Achaemenid Persia (539 B.C.E.–304 B.C.E.). The state of Achaemenid chronology was the subject of a series of studies published by this writer about ten to fifteen years ago. Newly emerged evidence has necessitated the present updates. Errata in those earlier studies are listed in an appendix. The focus of the present investigation is on what is new. A comprehensive statement on Achaemenid chronology that progresses from first principles and combines all that is new with all that is old remains desirable.

Few historical events are as transforming in the history of nations as the death of one ruler and the accession of the next. Accordingly, the chronology of regnal transitions deserves special attention in the study of ancient chronology. This essay provides updates for the chronology of nine regnal transitions in the Achaemenid empire: Xerxes I to Artaxerxes I (465); Artaxerxes I to Darius II (424-23); Darius II to Artaxerxes II (405/4); Artaxerxes II to Artaxerxes III (359/58); Artaxerxes III to Arses (338); Arses to Darius III (336/35); Darius III to Alexander III (331); Alexander III to Philip Arridaios (323); and Arridaios to Alexander IV (317). A comprehensive tabulation of the regnal years of the final years of the empire (340–304) has now become possible. It is presented at the end.

TABLE OF CONTENTS

Preface 1
   Statement of Purpose 1
   "Achaemenid" 3
   Babylonian Astronomy 4
   Dating Regnal Transitions 6
   "*Ca.*" 6
   Nature of the Updates 7
   Acknowledgments 8
1. From Xerxes I to Artaxerxes I (465) 9
2. From Artaxerxes I to Darius II (424–23) 13
   2.1. Main Events according to Ktesias of Knidos 13
   2.2. Three Problems 15
      2.2.1. Main Problem: Winter 425/24 B.C.E. or Winter 424/23 B.C.E.? 15
      2.2.2. Two Related Problems: Date of Artaxerxes I's Death
            and Date of Darius II's Accession 15
   2.3. Newly Emerged Evidence: Three Cuneiform Tablets 16
   2.4. Winter 425/24 B.C.E. or Winter 424/23 B.C.E.? 16
      2.4.1. Long Known Evidence in Favor of Winter 425/24 B.C.E.:
           The Greek Sources (Thucydides, Diodoros, and Ktesias) 16
      2.4.2. Long Known Evidence in Favor of Winter 424/23 B.C.E.:
           The Babylonian "Year 41" 17
      2.4.3. Artaxerxes I's Babylonian "Year 41" 17
          2.4.3.1. "Year 41": Fact or Fiction? 17
          2.4.3.2. The Return of "Year 41" in Double Dates of Darius II's Accession Year 18
          2.4.3.3. Kugler's Interpretation of the Return of "Year 41" as Evidence in Favor of
               425/24 B.C.E. 19
              Step one: Uniqueness of the Return of "Year 41" 19
              Step two: Unique Character of the Transition 19
              Step three: Length of Interval between Reigns
                   Uncertain and therefore Unusable 19
              Step four: Interval between Death and Return
                   of "Year 41" about a Year Long 19
              Step five: Possible Confusion in the Absence of "Year 41" 20
              Step six: Adding "Year 41" to Avoid Confusion 20

2.4.3.4. The Evidence for Kugler's Interpretation of the Return
of "Year 41": Posteriority of the Double Dates 20

2.4.3.5. *BE* X no. 5 as a Weak Link in Kugler's Interpretation
of "Year 41"'s Return 22

2.4.4. New Cuneiform Evidence in Favor of Winter 425/24 B.C.E.:
Artaxerxes I Died before the Total Eclipse of 4 Apr 424 B.C.E.
according to BM 34684 + 34787... 22

2.5. The Date of Artaxerxes I's Death:
A Day in *ca.* 26 Jan-*ca.* 16 Feb 424 B.C.E. 28

2.6. The Date of Darius II's Accession:
A Day in *ca.* 25 Dec 424 B.C.E.-*ca.* 10 Jan 423 B.C.E. 31

2.7. Xerxes II and Sekyndianos 31

2.8. Two Excursuses Involving Artaxerxes I and Darius II..................................... 32

2.8.1. Darius II's "Year 13" in Thucydides VIII 58 32

2.8.2. Day 1 of Judaism: 24 Tishri (*ca.* 30 Oct?) of 445 B.C.E. 33

3. From Darius II to Artaxerxes II (405/4) 35

4. From Artaxerxes II to Artaxerxes III (359/58) 37

5. From Artaxerxes III to Arses (338) 39

6. From Arses to Darius III (336/35) 41

7. From Darius III to Alexander III (332–30) 43

8. From Alexander III to Arridaios (323) 47

8.1. History of the Study of the Date of Alexander's Death 47

8.2. The Year:
Year 1 of Olympiad 114 or Olympiad CXIV.4 *(324/23* B.C.E.*)* 48

8.3. The Month and Part of Month:
*The Lunar Month Beginning around the Conjunction
of 12 May 323* B.C.E., *More Precisely Its End* 49

8.4. The (Half-)Day: *Daylight 11 Jun 323* B.C.E. 50

8.5. The Hour: *Perhaps rather* ca. *3:00–4:00 p.m.*
than ca. *4:00–5:00 p.m.* 50

9. From Arridaios to Alexander IV (317) 53

9.1. A Traditional Day-exact Date for the Death of Arridaios 53

9.2. Regnal Year Counts in Egypt and Babylon
in the Wake of Arridaios' Death down to 304 B.C.E. and
Their Relation to Political History 55

9.2.1. Counting Years in Daily Life and in Astronomy 55

9.2.2. Egypt 55

9.2.3. Babylon 56

9.2.3.1. Principal Characteristic 56

  9.2.3.2. 317 B.C.E.–315 B.C.E.: Arridaios, post-Arridaios,
    and early Alexander IV 56

  9.2.3.3. 317 B.C.E.–308 B.C.E.: Antigonos 57

  9.2.3.4. Antigonos' Years in Cuneiform Sources: Survey 58

  9.2.3.5. 311 B.C.E.–304 B.C.E.:
    The Later Alexander IV and Seleukos 59

10. How Did They Die? 61

11. Final Regnal Years of the Achaemenid Empire: Tabulation 63

Appendix I: Errata in Previous Publications 73

Appendix II: Remarks on Most Recent Publications 75

Abbreviations and References 81

Indices 87

1. Index of Passages Cited 87

  1.1. Aramaic Sources 87

  1.2. Bible Passages 87

  1.3. Cuneiform Sources 88

  1.4. Demotic Egyptian Sources 90

  1.5. Greek Sources 90

  1.6. Hieroglyphic Egyptian Sources. 92

  1.7. Latin Sources. 92

2. Index of Modern Authors Cited 93

3. Index of Subjects Treated 94

To the memory of Franz Xaver Kugler S.J.

Ombra mai fu . . . soave più.
Handel, *Serse*, Act 1, Scene 1

PREFACE

Statement of Purpose

In the house of history, chronology receives its fair share of attention. What remains wanting is a comprehensive treatment of all of chronology starting from first principles. Chronology is an intellectual structure whose elements come in a fixed logical order. Accordingly, something needs to be first. But such a comprehensive treatment, however desirable, far exceeds the scope of the present study. No small effort would be required to produce it.

Some parts of chronology pose greater challenges than others. On the whole, "BC" chronology is much more complex than "AD" chronology. The Julian calendar, instituted in 45 B.C.E. (B.C.) and still in use today, lends great transparency to "AD" chronology. The only topic of "AD" chronology posing significant problems is the earlier history of the computus, that is, the computation of Easter, which originates in the computation of the Passover. The present investigation is about "BC" chronology.

In relation to the larger context of "BC" chronology, the focus of the investigation is narrow in at least two respects. First, it concerns just one episode of "BC" chronology, namely the chronology of the Achaemenid Persian empire, here defined as lasting from 539 B.C.E. to 304 B.C.E. (see below). Second, the present investigation does not treat Achaemenid chronology from first principles. Rather, it furnishes updates to other investigations that do, more specifically a number of studies by the present author written ten to fifteen years ago (Depuydt 1995a, 1995b, 1995c, 1995d, 1996, and 1997). Ideally, a comprehensive statement on Achaemenid chronology including both all that is old and all that is new, with references to all past research on the matter, would be desirable. The pertinent data are scattered over countless books and articles published over many decades in several disciplines. Meanwhile, the focus of the present investigation may be narrow, but it is at least sharp.

Chronological disquisitions sometimes suffer from laconicity, which makes them accessible to no more than the initiated few, as if explicitness is in danger of appearing verbose. Then again, chronological arguments exhibit a certain deductive sequentiality in which every step is indispensable. In mathematics, theorems are repeated endlessly and no one ever complains. Then why would chronology be different?

Thirteen kings ruled the Achaemenid empire if one disregards ephemeral rulers: Cyrus, Cambyses, Darius I, Xerxes I, Artaxerxes I, Darius II, Artaxerxes II, Artaxerxes III, Arses (probably Artaxerxes [IV]), Darius III, Alexander III "the Great," Philip Arridaios, and Alexander IV. All of these kings except Cyrus were Pharaohs of Egypt. Nine ruled Egypt throughout their entire reign. Three ruled Egypt only for part of their reign: Cambyses a few years in the second half of his reign, Artaxerxes II a few years at the beginning of his reign, and Artaxerxes III only for some months at the end of his reign. Thirteen reigns involve thirteen beginnings and thirteen ends, together amounting to fourteen episodes, namely the beginning of the first reign, twelve transitions encompassing an end and a beginning, and the end of the thirteenth reign. The first reign begins with Cyrus' conquest of Babylon in 539 B.C.E. The end of the last reign is that of Alexander IV.

Of these fourteen episodes, eleven episodes including ten transitions of reign took place when Egypt was part of the Achaemenid empire. Three episodes including two transitions happened during Egyptian independence, namely Cyrus' conquest of Babylon in 539 B.C.E. (*PD* 14) and the two transitions from Cyrus to Cambyses in August 530 B.C.E. (*PD* 14) and from Artaxerxes II to Artaxerxes III in the period lasting from 26 Nov 359 B.C.E. to 10 Mar 358 B.C.E. (*PD* 19; see also §4 below).

Relying on information compiled in the afore-mentioned studies published ten to fifteen years ago, I recently described the dating of the seven transitions of reign that took place when Persia ruled Egypt for a chapter on Saite and Persian chronology (664 B.C.E.–332 B.C.E.) in the new handbook of Egyptian chronology (Depuydt 2006a [completed in 2002]: 266, 271–83). Five transitions are part of the First Persian Dominion of Egypt, which lasted from about 525 B.C.E. to about 400 B.C.E., as follows: (1)

Cambyses to Darius I (522); (2) Darius I to Xerxes I (486); (3) Xerxes I to Artaxerxes I (465); (4) Artaxerxes I to Darius II (424–23); and (5) Darius II to Artaxerxes II (405/4). Two transitions took place in the Second Persian Dominion, which lasted hardly six or seven years, from Artaxerxes III's re-conquest of Egypt (339/38 B.C.E.) to Alexander's conquest in 332 B.C.E., as follows: (6) from Artaxerxes III to Arses (338); (7) from Arses to Darius III (336/35). But in the absence of evidence, the afore-mentioned chapter in the handbook of Egyptian chronology lists only what Ptolemy's Royal Canon transmits about the reigns of Artaxerxes III, Arses, and Darius III.

When I recently returned to Achaemenid chronology, it appeared that the dating of five of the seven transitions just mentioned could be updated in major or minor ways, namely (3) to (7). In addition, so could the dating of four additional transitions of reign in the Achaemenid empire, namely: (1) Artaxerxes II to Artaxerxes III (359/58); (2) Darius III to Alexander III (331); (3) Alexander III to Philip Arridaios (323); and (4) Philip Arridaios to Alexander IV (317).

Presenting updates for the nine regnal transitions in question is the principal aim of this investigation. The anatomy of Achaemenid chronology in general and of Achaemenid-Egyptian chronology in specific, including the capital principle of predating of postdating, cannot be repeated in detail (see Depuydt 1995a–d, 1996, 2006a–b, with bibliographical references to earlier work). Nor can other facets of Achaemenid history be addressed. Achaemenid history has in recent times been the subject of many important inquiries. Suffice it to refer here to Briant's synthesis (2002 [1996]) and the 13 volumes that have appeared so far in the series *Achaemenid History* (1987–2003). I have not yet seen Kuhrt's internet sourcebook (2007).

The updates concern the *last* nine of the twelve transitions of reign that occurred in the sequence of thirteen kings listed above, as follows:

Xerxes I	to Artaxerxes I	(465)	(pp. 9–12)
Artaxerxes I	to Darius II	(424–23)	(pp. 13–34)
Darius II	to Artaxerxes II	(405/4)	(p. 35)
Artaxerxes II	to Artaxerxes III	(359/58)	(p. 37)
Artaxerxes III	to Arses	(338)	(p. 39)
Arses	to Darius III	(336/35)	(p. 41)
Darius III	to Alexander III	(331)	(pp. 41–46)
Alexander III	to Philip Arridaios	(323)	(pp. 47–51)
Philip Arridaios	to Alexander IV	(317)	(pp. 53–60)

Only in one of these nine transitions did Persia not rule Egypt, namely the one from Artaxerxes II to Artaxerxes III. In five of the nine transitions, the current best date range that includes the end of one reign and the beginning of the next belongs inside a period lasting one Julian year. In three more of the nine transitions, the transition can be dated inside a period lasting one Babylonian year. A Babylonian year straddles two Julian years and is therefore identified above by two Julian years separated by a slash (/). Babylonian years begin in the spring and consist of 12 or 13 lunar months of 29 or 30 days. Of any 100 lunar months, about 47 will contain 29 days and about 53 will contain 30 days. At some point, months and years were organized in Babylon into regular 19-year cycles each consisting of exactly 7 years of 13 lunar months and 12 years of 12 lunar months. Finally, in one of the nine transitions listed above, the En-dash (–) signifies a significant interval separating the end of one reign from the beginning of the next.

To my knowledge, no new evidence has come to light regarding the dating of the four earliest of the fourteen episodes defining the lengths of the thirteen reigns of the Achaemenid empire. The dates for the beginnings of the four reigns in question remain as before as follows.

start of Cyrus' rule of Babylon	*ca.* 29 Oct 539	(*PD* 14)
accession of Cambyses	Aug 530	(*PD* 14)
accession of Darius I	*ca.* 29 Sep–*ca.* 22 Dec 522	(Depuydt 1995b: 158)
accession of Xerxes I	late Nov 586	(Depuydt 1995b: 157–58)

Finally, as regards the last episode, the end of Alexander IV's reign, it has long been known that documents kept being dated fictionally to his reign even after his death in 310–309 B.C.E., until about 305/4 B.C.E.

"Achaemenid"

In or shortly before 525 B.C.E., the Persian ruler Cambyses (II) of the Achaemenid dynasty conquered Egypt after his father Cyrus (II) had conquered Babylon some years earlier in 539 B.C.E. The dynasty traces its origins to a legendary king Achaemenes, perhaps Cyrus' great-great-grandfather. Its ancestral homeland is the plain of Marv Dasht in Fārs in southwestern Iran, where the ruins of Persepolis and the modern city of Shiraz are located (Briant 2002 [1996]: 16–17). Cambyses' conquest was long placed in about mid-525 B.C.E., but I believe it to be better dated less precisely to 527 B.C.E.–525 B.C.E. (Depuydt 1996). As a result of this conquest, the capital cities of Susa, Babylon, and Memphis for the first time belonged to a single kingdom, the largest the world had ever seen (on its history, see now Briant 1997, 2001, and 2002 [1996]). The empire's unprecedented size left its mark on the Bible. Duly impressed, the author of the Biblical book of Esther describes Xerxes I (486 B.C.E.–465 B.C.E.) as "ruling from India to Ethiopia over one hundred twenty-seven provinces" (Esther 1:1).

With the Achaemenid empire as with any epoch, for example the Middle Ages, there is more than one way of defining beginning and end. The beginning of the Achaemenid empire is most commonly set at Cyrus' conquest of Babylon in 539 B.C.E. Babylon was the preeminent city in West Asia at the time and remained so even after the conquest. It is only after this conquest that Persia was more than just a strong nation and could now properly be called an empire. Alternatively, the beginning of the empire might be defined, not as a specific year, but rather as the period 539 B.C.E.–525 B.C.E. in order to include the conquest of Egypt, which gave the empire a territorial expanse never before seen.

If the empire is only Achaemenid when ruled by descendants of the legendary Achaemenes, then the defeat of Darius III at the battle of Gaugamela in the morning of 1 Oct 331 B.C.E. signifies the end of the empire. The Babylonian date of the battle is lunar Month 6 (Ululu) Day 24, as reported in cuneiform tablet B(ritish) M(useum) 36761, at ´Obv(erse)´ 15´–18´ (Sachs and Hunger 1988: 178–79). The symbol " ´ " marks the location of lost portions, for example, loss of the beginning in "´Rev(erse)," loss of the end in "Rev.´," and loss of both in "´Rev.´" (see ibid.: 39).

On the other hand, Alexander III "the Great" assumed command over the empire in the configuration that rulers of the Achaemenid dynasty had given it. Alexander III's half-brother Philip Arridaios (or Arrhidaios) and his son Alexander IV also ruled the same empire, even if only nominally. Generals were in control of the day-to-day affairs of the empire. The principal ones were Antigonos the One-Eyed and Seleukos, the later king Seleukos I, in Mesopotamia and Ptolemy, the later king Ptolemy I, in Egypt. Even after the death of Alexander IV some time in 310–309 B.C.E., regnal years were still counted by his fictitious reign for several years. It is only from 305/4 B.C.E. onward that Seleukos and Ptolemy styled themselves as "king" (*basileus*) without any reservations. Alexander III, Arridaios, and Alexander IV were not Achaemenids. Still, they ruled the Achaemenid empire, even if at some point only in name. They can therefore justifiably be included in a treatment of the empire's chronology. In order to include the last surviving semblance of the Achaemenid empire, its end may be dated to 304 B.C.E.

Historically and chronologically, Achaemenid Persia occupies a certain pivotal position in the history of the West (as for religiously, see §2.8.2). History begins with the earliest written sources, roughly about 3000 B.C.E. In 5000 years of history, different nations have occupied center stage. In the first half, until about 600/500 B.C.E., Egypt and Mesopotamia were most prominent. A shift occurred about halfway, around 500–300 B.C.E. The baton passed to the Classical world, as it were. Persia played a pivotal role in this shift. First, Persia united Egypt and Mesopotamia into a single empire, the largest the world had ever seen. Around 525 B.C.E., Cambyses conquered Egypt after Cyrus had earlier taken Babylon in 539 B.C.E. For the first time in history, the capital cities of Babylon and Memphis were now under one rule. The shift from the Near East to the Classical World, from Nile, Euphrates, and Tigris to the Mediterranean Sea, is epitomized by the Persian Wars. Early on in the shift, Persia could still challenge Greece on its own territory, even if suffering defeat at Marathon in 490 B.C.E. and at Salamis in 480 B.C.E. At the end of the shift, Alexander the Great conquered Persia.

Chronologically too, Achaemenid Persia is pivotal. The single most important chronological milestone in 5000 years of history is the onset of day-exact dating (Depuydt 2006b). From then on and not before, it is possible to determine the exact number of days that passed between a certain historical event and the present day. That number of days obviously increases by one day every day as time progresses. Day-exact dating securely begins in 664/3 B.C.E. in Egypt, some time in the Egyptian year lasting from 5 Feb 664 B.C.E. to 4 Feb 663 B.C.E., on the day on which Psammetichus I's reign began, whichever it was. But the Julian equivalent of the earliest datable historical event is 2 Mar 656 B.C.E., found in the Nitocris stela (Depuydt 2006b: 468–69). Until about 400 B.C.E., day-exact dating is unique to Egypt, except for many dates of astronomical events in Babylonian cuneiform tablets. In contrast to the discontinuous nature of day-exact dates from Babylonia, day-exact dating in Egypt is continuous in said period. It would also be continuous in Babylon if the preserved cuneiform record of texts of astronomical purport were more complete. After about 400 B.C.E., there is a disruption in Egypt's day-exact dating. Day-exact dating resumes in 359 B.C.E. The earliest period of day-exact dating in world history may be Egyptian, but it is ultimately based on evidence derived from Babylonian astronomical texts. This evidence cannot be set forth in detail here (cf. Depuydt 2008). It is a singularly fortunate circumstance, as it were, for the cause of ancient chronology that Cambyses conquered Egypt. The earliest period of day-exact dating is in part owed to the fact that events in both Egypt and Babylon came to be dated to the same ruler from the conquest onward. This overlap and intertwining of cultures made it possible for Babylonian astronomy to shed light on Egyptian chronology. By one calculation, equations of Egyptian dates with Babylonian dates in Aramaic papyri from Egypt leave only one chance in about eight trillion that our understanding of ancient chronology from fifth-century B.C.E. onwards is fundamentally flawed (Depuydt 2007: 60).

Babylonian Astronomy

One subject that will not be updated here is Babylonian astronomy. Babylonian astronomy is the Alpha of "BC" chronology. Any increase in understanding of Babylonian astronomy therefore strengthens the chronology of the period "BC" and especially of the chronology of the first millennium B.C.E. Among the authors of recent contributions to the subject are Lis Brack-Bernsen, John Britton, Hermann Hunger, Olaf Pedersen, David Pingree, and John Steele. A review of recent developments exceeds the scope of the present investigation. Suffice it to refer to the two recent collections of articles edited by Steele (2007) and Ross (2008) (see also Swerdlow 1999 and Steele and Imhausen 2002). The bibliography found in these contributions should lead to much if not most else that is important.

Cuneiform astronomy exhibits much more complexity than hieroglyphic astronomy. Still, both are better deemed pre-scientific. Both lack a crucial ingredient that would make them truly scientific. The language of physical sciences such as astronomy, their final truth as it were, consists of numbers. The numbers of astronomy are those of trigonometry. Most of the numbers of trigonometry are irrational, for example, the square root of two divided by two. There is no trace in either hieroglyphic or cuneiform sources of irrational numbers. Hipparchus of Rhodes discovered trigonometry in the second century B.C.E. As the real distances between stars were not known, trigonometry operated with the *proportions* between distances and angles. For example, a pole raised at one end from a horizontal position reaches *half* of its maximal height after having traversed a *third* of the 90 degree angle. One says that the sinus of 30 degrees is 0.5. The length of the pole is irrelevant. What matters is the relation between the distance and the angle as a mathematical function. In that sense, the numbers of Babylonian astronomy are, for all their sophistication, merely approximate.

The crowning achievement of Babylonian astronomy is its lunar theory. Which observations could serve as the foundation of a lunar theory? In the absence of the true foundations of astronomy, namely trigonometry, Babylonian astronomers had to rely on what they saw. In that sense, the most striking empirical characteristic of the moon is its relation to the sun.

Preface

The sun and the moon are like two runners chasing one another roughly on the same path in the sky. The moon is losing its race with the sun, as it were. Every day, the sun rushes ahead of the moon or the moon falls behind the sun by about 12 degrees. The sun catches up again with the moon after between 29 and 30 days.

The most precisely timeable *events* in this chase are when sun or moon cut the horizon by either rising up from the eastern horizon or by sinking below the western horizon. Accordingly, the most precisely measurable *intervals* of time are those between either moonrise or moonset and either sunrise or sunset. These intervals can of course be measured at any time of the month. But the Babylonians soon came to regard six limit intervals as the most interesting. These are intervals between two horizon crossings of sun and moon that can be seen and measured for the first time after or the last time before an absence. They are observed when sun and moon are as close as possible to one another in the same horizon, east or west, or as far away as possible from one another in either horizon. There are six intervals in total. All are measured in *uš*. Each *uš* lasts about four minutes.

When the sun and moon are close to one another in the same horizon, the sun is in fact just catching up with the moon. Two intervals apply, with interval (2) following interval (1) after about three days: (1) (in the east in the morning, with the moon still ahead) the interval between moonrise and sunrise the last time the moon is seen rising in front of the sun, called KUR in cuneiform; (2) (in the west in the evening, with the moon now behind) the interval between sunset and moonset the first time the moon is seen setting behind the sun, called *na* in cuneiform.

When the moon is at one end of the sky and the sun at the other, four intervals apply. Each interval combines a rising and a setting. At some point, the moon drops to 180 degrees behind the sun. The sun is then also 180 degrees behind the moon. Two of the intervals apply before the moon has fallen 180 degrees behind. When the moon is still closer than 180 degrees to the sun, the sun is more than 180 degrees behind the moon. Accordingly, the moon wins the race to either horizon in order to either rise or set, as it were. Drawing a little diagram to visualize the matter is always useful. Moonrise therefore still precedes sunset and moonset still precedes sunrise. The size of these two intervals the *last* time that they can still be seen and measured are denoted by the cuneiform signs ME and ŠÚ. After the moon has fallen more than 180 degrees behind, it is the sun that wins the same race to the horizon. Now sunrise precedes moonset and sunset precedes moonrise. The size of the two intervals the *first* time they can be seen and measured are denoted by the cuneiform signs *na* and GE_6. The term *na* is used for two of the six intervals. In both cases, the moon sets and cuts the horizon soon after the sun. Once the sun is setting before the moon in the same horizon, the other time the sun is rising before the moon at the opposite horizon.

The Babylonians meticulously observed these six intervals over several centuries. Gradually, patterns emerged and a theory was developed (see Brack-Bernsen 1997). But absent an adequate conception of the solar system and Newton's laws, the Babylonians never grasped the deeper causes of these patterns. Absent trigonometry, they never penetrated to the exact numbers that represent the final truth of these patterns. The numbers of their lunar theory are therefore all approximations. Certain numbers are remarkably accurate. An example is 29 days 12 hours 44 minutes 3⅓ seconds for the average length of the lunar month. That is less than one second removed from the real average length. Lunar months otherwise range in length from around 29 days 6½ hours to around 29 days 20 hours. However, the precision of the Babylonian average does not result directly from Babylonian lunar theory. It rather results from meticulous observations over many centuries. It is simply the result of dividing a great distance in time between two lunar eclipses of similar type by the number of lunar months that separate the two eclipses. Eclipses can be timed fairly precisely. An error in timing of as much as an hour or 3600 seconds is reduced to less than a second if an average lunar month is obtained for a period that lasts more than 3600 lunar months or close to three centuries. Again, the high degree of precision of the Babylonian average lunar month is therefore owed to meticulous observation over many centuries rather than to an explicit theory.

Dating Regnal Transitions

A transition of reign is potentially a complex historical and political event with a certain extension in time. No transition is quite like any other. Yet when the typical scenario applies, few events are as sharply definable in chronological terms. Typically, a king dies and the heir apparent is instantly recognized as ruler. Such a transition has no extension in time. It happens from one moment to the next. Death is the event that defines all. The transformation of the king's body from a breathing entity to a lifeless corpse can in principle be measured almost to the second.

That split second event marks both the end of one reign and the beginning of the next, even if a formal accession ceremony may take place only later. An example. According to the Babylonian Chronicle, Nabopolassar died on Month 5 Day 8 in 605 B.C.E., that is, *ca.* 15 August in that Julian year (*PD* 12). Nebuchadrezzar formally ascended the throne 22 or 23 days later on Month 6 Day 1, that is, *ca.* 7 September. However, if the succession was uncontested, Nebuchadrezzar *de facto* ruled the minute Nabopolassar died. When a succession is not settled, a gap separates the end of one reign and the beginning of the next. Two moments in time, not just one, need to be dated. All departures from the typical scenario of succession exhibit their own distinctive characteristics. Each requires its own treatment as to what constitutes the end of one reign and the beginning of the next.

Death is an unusual event with regard to both chronology and history. Chronologically, it often marks both the end of one period and the beginning of the next. Historically, especially in the case of a natural death, there is a characteristic sharp contrast between the passivity of dying and the flurry of activity that follows it.

Of only three of the thirteen Achaemenid rulers is the exact day of death known with some probability. They are Xerxes I, Alexander III, and Arridaios (see §§1, 8, and 9). In addition, the battle of Gaugamela in the morning of 1 Oct 331 B.C.E. may be styled as the last day of Darius III's reign even if his life did not end on that day. As regards the other regnal transitions, no date is preserved in the surviving sources that can be identified as last day of the reign or as first of the next reign. Instead, the interval of time will need to be determined within which power may be deemed to have passed completely from one stable ruler to the next. Typically, that interval begins with the latest known date for one ruler and ends with the earliest known date of the next ruler. But other special considerations may apply.

"Ca."

The qualifier "*ca.*" as a rule accompanies the Julian equivalents of Babylonian lunar dates. That is because Julian equivalents of lunar dates may be off by one or two days—unless a lunar month and day date is fixed astronomically in some way. For about eight centuries, from the mid-eighth century B.C.E. to the mid-first century C.E., astronomers of the city of Babylon recorded celestial events. Over time, their careful observations came to serve as the basis of astronomical theories. It is to this day the longest research project in history ever. There are close to 10,000 lunar months in the long period in question. The astronomers fixed the length of each lunar month at either 29 days or 30 days and kept a complete record of all those lengths. In order to calculate the distance in days between two astronomical events, they needed to know how long each month had been. An error of just a single day is impermissible. An example of a cuneiform tablet that lists the lengths of all the lunar months in a period of 32 years is BM 32337 (see now Hunger 2001: 100–109 [no. 39]). At Babylon, the scribes of business documents and colophons in literary manuscripts may well have used the same month lengths as the city's astronomers.

Many if not most of the records of month-lengths have been lost. It would be convenient to have a published list of all the lunar months that can be dated exactly. In some cases, the exact Julian equivalent of Day 1 is known but it is not known whether the month had 29 days or 30 days. The dating of the month is then day-exact up to Day 29, unless the beginning of the next month is known exactly.

PD lists the Julian dates of the beginnings of all the Babylonian lunar months in the period from 626 B.C.E to 75 C.E. However, all the Julian dates "have been calculated by the new-moon tables of Karl Schoch" (p. 25). These Julian dates either coincide with the historical date or are hardly more than one day off. In other words, it is not certain that they are the exact Julian dates, to the very day, of the beginnings of the Babylonian lunar months. Yet, all these beginnings must have been part of the ancient record. If the entire record had been preserved, then we would know the exact Julian equivalent of the beginning of every lunar month over a period of eight centuries. As it happens, only a small portion of the record has survived. In many instances, the Julian date of Day 1 of the month can be inferred with certainty. Such is the case with the dates of astronomical events such as eclipses. For example, if the Babylonian date of a lunar eclipse in the middle of a month is known, then the Julian date of Day 1 of the lunar month can be inferred with certainty.

Again, it would be desirable to have a complete listing of all that is known of Babylonian lunar months to the exact day in Julian terms. That is the day-exact part of Babylonian chronology. The day-exact part amounts to only a small portion of the entire period of eight centuries. Ninety years ago, in a perceptive and lucid study surveying what was known at the time about Assyrian and Babylonian chronology in the wake of the decipherments of astronomical tablets by Julius Epping, Franz Xaver Kugler, and Johan Strassmaier, Sidersky (1916: 46 [150]–57 [161]) compiled 657 equivalences of correspondences between Julian dates and Babylonian dates. These equivalences would cover about 6½% of all the lunar months in the period between 747 B.C.E. and 75 C.E. This number is obtained as follows. There are 821 years in that period. Since there are about 365.2422 days in a year and an average of about 29.53059 days in a lunar month, there are 12.37 (365.2422 : 29.53059) lunar months in a year and therefore close to 10,154 lunar months in 821 years. The 657 instances amount to about 6½% of these. Sidersky anticipated that (p. 59) the gaps in his table "seront probablement comblées peu à peu par le déchiffrement d'autres inscriptions astronomiques conservées dans les musées."

However, it is not clear how Sidersky obtained each of his equivalences. He carefully cites the publications from which he derived them, but not the ways in which each of the equivalences were obtained. It appears that the Julian dates are not always associated with what has turned out to be the actual ancient date. An example. In Sidersky's table (1916: 50), the Babylonian calendar year that encompasses both Alexander's Year 14 and—from his death on 11 Jun 323 B.C.E.—Arridaios' Year 1 begins on (the evening preceding daylight of) 15 April, as it does in the tables in *PD*, at p. 36. However, since the publication of BM 45766 (Sachs and Hunger 1988: 204–7), it is known that the year in question rather began in Babylonian astronomical texts on (the evening preceding daylight of) *14* April (Sachs and Hunger 1988: 218), a day earlier. The date of 15 April in *PD* is obtained by computation (*PD* 25). Presumably, Sidersky obtained 15 April likewise by computation. The fact is that the association of daylight of Month 1 (Nisanu) Day 1 with daylight of 15 Apr 323 B.C.E. does not accord with historical fact as derived from tablets that have emerged since. By contrast, the association of daylight of Month 1 Day 1 with daylight of 14 Apr 323 B.C.E. is now final. Such finality would be desirable for every month in a period spanning eight centuries. It is doubtful that such a comprehensive statement will ever be possible. Meanwhile, it remains to be established to how many of the almost 10,000 lunar months in that period such finality does apply.

Sidersky's table is not a record of all firm associations between Julian dates and Babylonian dates, contrary to what it may appear to be at first sight. In fact, Sidersky obtains many of his dates by assuming (1916: 44) that "[l]e *Saros-Canon* . . . nous a fourni les dates de Nisanu et d'autres mois d'un grand nombre d'années." However, the Saros-Canon only gives the lunar months in which eclipses are deemed possible. One still needs to observe the sky to establish whether an eclipse actually materializes. What is more, the Canon does *not* give the exact day of the eclipse, typically Day 14 or Day 15. If it had, the *exact* Julian date of Day 1 of the month could have been inferred.

Nature of the Updates

The updates presented below are of different types. In regard to six of the nine transitions (§§1, 2, 4, 5, 6, and 9), the updates involve increased precision in dating. In regard to two of these six transitions, Xerxes I to Artaxerxes I (465) (§1) and Arses to Darius III (336/35) (§6), the increase in precision amounts to *days only*. But for the latter transition, there is an additional possibility that the increase involves *several months*. In regard to the beginning of the reign of Darius II that is part of a third transition, Artaxerxes I to Darius II (424–23) (§2), as well as in regard to a fourth transition, Artaxerxes II to Artaxerxes III (359/58) (§4), the increase in precision amounts to *about a month*. In regard to a fifth transition, Arridaios to Alexander IV (317) (§9), the increase in precision amounts to a *couple of months*. It is in regard to a sixth transition, Artaxerxes III to Arses (338) (§5), that the imprecision is reduced the most, namely from a year to just a month.

One update to a transition involves a decrease in precision in dating. In regard to one transition, Artaxerxes I to Darius II (424–23) (§2), a recalibration in light of new evidence widens rather than narrows, namely by some days, the margin of uncertainty for the date of the end of the reign of Artaxerxes I.

In regard to three of the eight transitions (§§2, 3, and 7), the update concerns something other than greater precision in dating, namely more refined conclusions pertaining in one way or another to tools of time-reckoning used by the Babylonians. The focus is on three such tools: (1) highly unusual double year dates found in certain cuneiform tablets; (2) the Babylonian accession year; (3) the counting of regnal years.

First, in regard to one transition, Artaxerxes I to Darius II (424–23 B.C.E.) (§2), the focus is on unusual double year dates. Evidence derived from three newly accessible cuneiform tablets makes it possible to reaffirm that Artaxerxes I had died in early 424 B.C.E. and not months later. Second, in regard to two more transitions, Darius II to Artaxerxes II (405/4) (§3) and Darius III to Alexander (§7), the focus is on the Babylonian accession year, MU.SAG in Babylonian. The accession year is the numberless period at the beginning of the reign of a Babylonian king lasting from his accession to the first new year in the spring. Newly accessible tablets positively confirm what had already been universally assumed, namely that Artaxerxes II had had one, and also what had been strongly suspected, that Alexander the Great did too. Also in regard to the transition from Darius III to Alexander (331) (§7), the focus is on how Alexander III's regnal years are counted in Egypt, Mesopotamia, and Ptolemy's Royal Canon. A comprehensive statement has now finally become possible.

A final update is *wissenschaftsgeschichtlich*. It concerns Alexander's date of death (323) (§8).

Acknowledgments

To Carl Olof Jonsson I owe certain references cited in recent articles of his (cf. also Jonsson 2004). He also read an advanced draft of the present essay and contributed useful comments. The references in question are to the following items: (1) the two cuneiform tablets Bertin 2889—whose date was first read by Francis Joannès and relayed to Jonsson by Jean-Frédéric Brunet in a message of 22 Dec 2003—and BM 54557; (2) an unpublished manuscript by George Bertin (1883) and Zawadzki's (1995–96) publication of BM 54557; (3) three double dates on tablets from Uruk and Babylon and in an Aramaic papyrus from Wadi Daliyeh along with pertinent statements about them by Boiy (2002a), Gropp (2001), Stolper (1999), and von Weiher (1998).

1. From Xerxes I to Artaxerxes I (465)

Essence of the Update.—(1) The date of the murder of Xerxes I can be reduced with high probability from being an uncertain day in a period lasting five days to the exact day, lunar Month 5 Day 14 in 465 B.C.E., that is, probably 4 August, much less likely 3 August or 5 August. (2) The two tablets CBS 10059 and AUWE 13 no. 307 shed light on certain facets of the transition without adding precision to its dating. (3) Xerxes I becomes one of only five Pharaohs whose date of death is day-exact, that is, can be measured from the present moment in time back into the past in terms of an exact number of days. Arridaios joins this company of five in another of the present updates (see §9).

It had been known for some time from eclipse text BM 32234 that the event described in that cuneiform tablet as ⌈Ḫi-ši?⌉-ár-šú DUMU-šú GAZ-šú "Xerxes (I), his son murdered him" happened on a day in the five-day period lasting in Babylonian lunar Month 5 (IZI or *Abu*) from Day 14 to 18 in 465 B.C.E. (Hunger 2001: 20–21 [no. 4]; *PD* 17; cf. Depuydt 2006a: 278 and 282 note xvii). The readings 4, 5, 6, 7, and 8 were all deemed equally possible for the damaged second sign of the two signs used to write the day number, the sign denoting the units. Two recent developments are that Walker (1997: 21 with 25 note 11; cf. Stolper 1999: 1) reexamined the number in question, deeming the day number "almost certainly to be 14," and that Hunger (2001: 16–21 [no. 4], at 21) in his publication of the text chooses 14 while leaving a question-mark. Both scholars apparently looked long and hard at this number and one wonders whether additional examination could bring further gain.

Several classical authors describe Xerxes I's murder, but there is much variation in the details of their accounts (Briant 2002 [1996]: 563–67, 970–71). These accounts agree for the most part that Xerxes' oldest son, who is called Darius, played a role in the events surrounding the murder. But they also agree that he was not the murderer. Rather, Xerxes' actual killer, the chief bodyguard Artabanos, convinced Xerxes' youngest son Artaxerxes that his brother Darius killed their father. Artaxerxes therefore had Darius put to death. Like the Babylonian eclipse text cited above, Aelian (*Varia historica,* XIII 3) transmits without further comment that Xerxes was killed by his own son. Perhaps, either or both of these sources took the false rumors spread by Artabanos as fact. "In the Babylonian tablets," writes Briant (2002 [1996]: 566), "Artaxerxes succeeds his father, with no break in continuity." The tablets in question are those listed in *PD* 17 (Briant 2002 [1996]: 971). Yet, the continuity is not as "unbroken" as when an explicit expression like *ina* AŠ-TE TUŠ-*ab* "he sat on the throne" refers to the succession, as it does in the eclipse text BM 71537 to the accessions of Artaxerxes III and Arses (Artaxerxes IV) (see §§4 and 5). The absence of such an expression leaves room for assuming, in accordance with what some sources seem to suggest, that Artaxerxes I did not ascend to the throne immediately. The earliest date of Artaxerxes I's reign remains one that is found, not in a cuneiform tablet, but in an Aramaic papyrus from Egypt (Porten 1990: 21, "C 6") dated to Month 9 Day 18 of "Year 21, accession year of Artaxerxes I," that is, *ca.* 2 Jan 464 B.C.E. According to *PD* 17, no known cuneiform tablets dated to the reign of Artaxerxes I are earlier than about mid-464 B.C.E.

Two other cuneiform tablets also shed light on the dating of the same transition. First, CBS 10059, a tablet from Nippur published by Stolper (1999: 1–2), was written apparently six days after Xerxes I was murdered. It is dated to Month 5 Day 20 of his Year 21. Presumably, news of the murder had not yet reached Nippur. Another case in which news apparently arrived with some delay at Nippur is discussed below (§2.5). Second, a newly emerged tablet, AUWE 13 no. 307 (von Weiher 1998: 123–24; cf. Stolper 1999: 3) contains the double date "Year 21, accession year of Artaxerxes I." The day number is 18, but the month name is lost.

What does it mean to call the date of death of Xerxes I and that of four other Pharaohs day-exact? Absolute certainty is too much to hope for. Instead, it means that a certain day-exact date has come into focus that can be defended on the basis of an explicit rationale as being the day in question with a high degree of probability. That is more than can be said about all the other Pharaohs of Egypt. Chronology is part of history. It is subject to the historical method, which asks among other things by which criteria one should or should not believe a statement found in an ancient source. The historical method often requires calibrating probabilities. The evidence is of so many different kinds that no historical problem is quite like any other. There are five day-exact dates of death of Pharaohs and each requires separate treatment. The five Pharaohs in question were either foreigners or of foreign origin. Psammetichus II must have been of Libyan stock. Xerxes I was a Persian. Alexander III and Arridaios were Macedonians and Ptolemy VIII Euergetes II was of Macedonian origin.

The case for Alexander (*d.* 11 Jun 323) seems to exhibit the highest degree of probability because it is supported by more than one reliable source (Depuydt 1997). The cases for the four other Pharaohs rely on a single statement and illustrate that the principle of the historical method known as *Testis unus testis nullus* "One witness is no witness" cannot be applied to ancient history without rejecting much of what we think we know. All four testimonies, two hieroglyphic and two cuneiform, occur in public and not private documents. The medium through which they have been transmitted indicates that they were recorded and inscribed with great care. It is difficult to think of any motive for deliberate falsification in any of the four cases. It is otherwise difficult to rank the probabilities of these four cases in terms of degree of veracity. Perhaps the two dates preserved in hieroglyphic sources are more probably day-exact than those preserved in cuneiform sources.

Only the earliest case, Psammetichus II's (*d.* 9 Feb 589), is completely free of explicit problems. A stela dedicated to his daughter, a God's Wife Ankhnesneferibre, states: *rnpt-sp 7 ʒbd 1 ʒḥt sw 23 pr nṯr pn . . . psmṯk r pt* "Year 7, Month 1 of the *ʒḥt*-season (first month of the year), Day 23, this god . . . Psammetichus went up to heaven" (Maspero 1904). Why would this statement be wrong?

The source for Ptolemy VIII Eurgetes II's case (*d.* 28 Jun 116) is no less than an inscription on the venerable temple of Horus at Edfu (Chassinat 1932: 9,3–4). It is difficult to see how the event described as and dated to *ḥʒt-sp 54 nt nsw pn 2.nw n šmw sw 11* "Regnal year 54 of this king, Month 2 of the *šmw* season (that is, Month 6) Day 11" can be read much differently than *wp bjk ḏnḥwy.f(y) r pt* "the falcon opened his wings toward heaven" and interpreted other than as a reference to the death of Ptolemy VIII Euergetes II. The statement that immediately follows confirms that a transition of reign is concerned: (sic) *sʒ.f wr dy.f s(w) ḥr ns(t).f* "As for his eldest son, he placed him on his throne." Month 6 Day 11 of Ptolemy VIII's Year 54 is 28 June 116 B.C.E. The only element of uncertainty is introduced by documents dated to Ptolemy VIII's reign after his presumed death on Month 6 Day 11 of his Year 54 (Skeat 1969: 35; Pestman 1967: 65). But because these dates fall less than a month later, it may be assumed that the news of the king's death reached many cities and towns of Egypt with a certain delay. If so, Ptolemy VIII Euergetes II's date of death seems to be as probably true as Psammetichus II's.

The two dates transmitted in cuneiform tablets pose explicit problems. The first problem pertains to the state of the text. The text of both reports is fragmentary. In the case of Xerxes I, the day number is damaged, as was noted above. But the reading is almost certainly 14. At least, the focus is now on one specific day as being much more probable than any other. In the case of Arridaios, the date is fully preserved and enough of the name has survived to make certain that Arridaios is meant. But what Arridaios exactly did on the date in question is lost. It is virtually certain, however, from certain arguments that what he did is die. The case is discussed in full in §9 below.

The second problem pertains to the nature of the calendar. In the case of Psammetichus II and Ptolemy VIII Euergetes II, the Egyptian calendar is used. This calendar is day-exact back to at least 664 B.C.E. (Depuydt 2006b). But the deaths of Xerxes I and Arridaios are dated by the Babylonian calendar, which is lunar. Two problems result from the use of this calendar.

The first problem is that modern estimates of the beginning of an ancient lunar month may be off by one or two days, unless special circumstances apply. In the case of Arridaios, however, the date is astronomically fixed to the exact day in another manner (see §9). In the case of Xerxes I, the date is not astronomically fixed but the text itself is astronomical in nature and the range of uncertainty is smaller in the case of lunar months in Babylonian astronomical texts than for lunar months in any other kind of text because much is known about when lunar days begin in that type of text. This knowledge is reflected in the computations of the beginnings of lunar months in *PD*. According to *PD*, Month 5 Day 14 corresponds to 4 August in 465 B.C.E. Accordingly, Month 5 Day 1 is 22 Jul 465 B.C.E. Such simple conversions can be securely achieved in the following manner.

	Julian		*Babylonian*	
	8/4	=	5/14	
–3				*–3*
	8/1	=	**5/11**	
–1				*–1*
	7/31	=	**5/10**	
–9				*–9*
	7/22	=	**5/1**	

The subtractions in italics are primary. An equal number of days is subtracted in the other column. The results are marked in bold.

The distance in time between sunset and moonset in the evening before daylight of Day 1 was an interval determined every month by Babylonian astronomers, whether it was observed or computed. Accordingly, that interval would have been determined for the evening of 21 Jul 465 B.C.E. Conjunction—the moment in time when sun, moon, and earth, in that order, are found on a single line or, better, in a single plane—was 20 July at 1:30 a.m. This is Goldstine's time (1973: 45), still sufficiently accurate for historical purposes and computed for Babylon, as it happens. The interval between sunset and moonset should have grown sufficiently for the first crescent to be seen by the evening of 21 July.

The question remains: Could daylight of 21 Jul 465 B.C.E. be daylight of lunar Day 1 and the day of Xerxes I's murder therefore 3 August? The interval between sunset and moonset would then need to be determined for the evening of 20 July. The distance in time from conjunction at 1:30 a.m. on July 20 would be about three quarters of day. A similar interval, only slightly larger, is attested for the evening of the day of Alexander's death, 11 Jun 323 B.C.E. He died on Month 2 (Aiaru) Day 29. The next day was Month 3 (Simanu) Day 1. In this case, the distance in time from conjunction at 0:06 a.m. on June 11 (Goldstine 1973: 57) to the evening of 11 June was also about three quarters of a day, in fact a little less. My general impression is that such short intervals tend to occur less often in the seventh to fifth centuries B.C.E., although not much evidence remains (Sachs and Hunger 1988: 42–65). They seem more common for later centuries. On the provisional assumption that an interval of three quarters of a day is too short for the fifth century B.C.E., 4 Aug 465 B.C.E. remains the preferred date for the death of Xerxes I.

The second problem is the conversion of lunar dates. Lunar months probably did not begin on the exact same day everywhere in Mesopotamia. Accordingly, if the death occurred elsewhere and was reported by the month and day number of the local calendar, the day with the same number in the calendar of Babylon might denote a day that is one or two days off and the conversion would result in a different day. The case of Arridaios is discussed in §9. Apparently, he was murdered far from Babylon and Susa in Greece. In the case of Xerxes I, the death may have occurred at Susa. Walker (1997: 23–24) has noted that there is a remarkable coincidence in dating between Babylon and Persepolis (and hence presumably also Susa, which is closer to Babylon) in regard to the placement of intercalary months. Babylonian astronomers were capable of determining lengths of months beforehand. Was there then perfect synchrony between Susa, Persepolis, and Babylon in that respect around the time of Xerxes I's death? The matter awaits further investigation.

These two problems make the day-exact dates of death of Xerxes I and Arridaios somewhat less certain than those of Psammetichus II and Ptolemy VIII Euergetes II. In favor of Arridaios' case and against

Xerxes I's case is that the former's Babylonian date of death is astronomically fixed. In favor of Xerxes I's case and against Arridaios' case is that Xerxes I died closer to Babylon or Susa. But at least, there is one day that seems more probable than any other. And the actual day, if not that one, must have been very close, perhaps no more than one or two days away.

The distance in exact full number of days from the hour and minute of each of the five rulers' deaths, whatever it was, to the same hour and minute day on 1 Jan 2009 C.E. (A.D.) is given below. I have used the Schrams' tables (Schram 1908). Each date is accompanied by its Julian day ("j.d.") number, according to a count that begins on 1 Jan 4713 B.C.E. Julian day numbers are cardinal. The first day of the j.d. count therefore lasts from j.d. 0.00 to j.d. 1.00. Noon of that day is j.d. 0.50. The j.d. number of "0" Feb 589 B.C.E. is 1,506,321. 9 Feb 589 B.C.E., listed below, is therefore strictly speaking 1,506,330, that is, lasts from 1,506,330.00 to 1,506,331.00. Noon of 9 Feb 589 B.C.E. is 1,506,330.50. However, Julian day numbers are converted into ordinal numbers below. The day that lasts cardinally from 1,506,330.00 to 1,506,331.00 is ordinally the 1,506,331st of the count, just as the day that lasts from j.d. 0.00 to j.d. 1.00 is the first.

Since Psammetichus II's death is the earliest exactly dated of any ancient ruler, it follows that no exact day of death of any ancient ruler is at present time earlier than a million days ago. But one will be by 2150 C.E.

		j.d. number (from 1 Jan 4713 B.C.E.), styled ordinally	days elapsed till 1 Jan 2009 C.E. (j.d. 2454834 ordinally)
Psammetich II	(*d.* 9 Feb 589 = Month 1 Day 23 Year 7 [Egypt.])	1,506,331th	948,503
Xerxes I	(*d.* 4 Aug 465 = Month 5 Day 14 Year 21 [Babyl.])	1,551,799th	903,035
Alexander III	(*d.* 11 Jun 323 = Month 2 Day 29 Year 14 [Babyl.])	1,603,610th	851,224
Arridaios	(*d.* 26 Dec 317 = Month 9 Day 27 Year 7 [Babyl.])	1,605,999th	848,834
Ptolemy VIII	(*d.* 28 June 116 = Month 6 Day 11 Year 54 [Egypt.])	1,679,234th	775,600

2. FROM ARTAXERXES I TO DARIUS II (424–23)

Essence of the Update.—Evidence derived from two recently published cuneiform tablets from Babylon—BM 34684 + 34787 (Hunger 2001: 34–38 [no. 9]) and BM 54557 (Zawadzki 1995–96)—as well as from the unpublished tablet Bertin 2889 (see Bertin 1883), also from Babylon, adds support and precision to three tenets already defended elsewhere. The three tenets can be reformulated and refined as follows:

(1) Artaxerxes I died in early 424 B.C.E. in his Babylonian Year 40 but documents kept being dated fictionally by his Year 40 and then by his Year 41 at least until late December 424 B.C.E. and possibly into the very first days of 423 B.C.E. The three afore-mentioned tablets—BM 34684 + 34787, BM 54557 and Bertin 2889—each in their own way provide new evidence in support of this tenet, as follows. BM 54557 makes a minor contribution to affirming winter 425/24 B.C.E. as opposed to winter 424/23 B.C.E. as the time of death. BM 34684 + 34787 provides a *terminus ante quem* "time before which," namely the total lunar eclipse of 4 Apr 424 B.C.E. Bertin 2889, in addition to making a contribution similar to that of BM 54557, also further delimits the period defined in (2).

(2) The end of Artaxerxes I's reign was acknowledged in the city of Babylon, most probably by a report of the date of his death in the historical and astronomical records, on a day in the period lasting

> *from Babylonian lunar Month 11 Day 4 to Month 11 Day 25 in early 424 B.C.E.,*
> *that is, ca. 26 Jan–ca. 16 Feb 424 B.C.E., both dates inclusive.*

Only tablets from the city of Babylon are used here to obtain these dates, whereas either tablets from both Nippur and Babylon or tablets from just Nippur were used in past calibrations. Bertin 2889 is added here to the tablets already used in earlier calibrations.

(3) The beginning of Darius II's reign was acknowledged in the city of Babylon on a day in the period lasting

> *from Babylonian lunar Month 9 Day 13 in late 424 B.C.E. until Babylonian lunar Month 9 Day 29 in early*
> *423 B.C.E.,that is, ca. 25 Dec 424 B.C.E.–ca. 10 Jan 423 B.C.E., both dates inclusive.*

The acknowledgment may have occurred a little earlier if news of the end of Artaxerxes I's Year 41 reached Nippur from Babylon with some delay. BM 54557 has allowed additional refinement of the date of the beginning of Darius II's reign.

2.1. Main Events according to Ktesias of Knidos

A century after Cambyses' conquest of Egypt made Achaemenid Persia into an empire and a century before Alexander's death led to its breakup, the most troubled and most storied regnal transition in the history of the Persian empire took place from the death of Artaxerxes I (465 B.C.E.–424 B.C.E.) to the accession of Darius II (424/23 B.C.E.–405/4 B.C.E.) (on this period in its larger historical context, see recently Stolper 1994: 237–38). There has been much discussion as to whether Artaxerxes I died either in or close to the winter of 425/24 B.C.E. or in or close to the winter of 424/23 B.C.E.

There is only one substantial report of what happened when Artaxerxes I died. That report is part of a history of Persia written in Greek by Ktesias of Knidos, the *Persika* (Περσικά). The *Persika* only survive in fragments quoted by later authors. König (1972) has collected and translated them. The passages pertaining to the transition from the reign of Artaxerxes I to the reign of Darius II are found in long excerpts cited by the Byzantine patriarch Photios (ninth century C.E.), namely §§43–49 in König's edition (1972: 17–19).

Ktesias' reputation as a historian is not among the best. That may have to do with the fact that much if not most of his *Persika* transmits legends of the past. Then again, Ktesias may well have accurately reported what he found in the archives of the Persian empire which, according to Diodoros (II 32), he says he carefully studied (König 1972: 161–62). In any event, what Ktesias says about a long-gone mythical past cannot be evaluated in the same way as his descriptions of events that took place in his own life-time.

In terms of the three coordinates time, place, and person, Ktesias could hardly have been closer to the events surrounding Artaxerxes I's death. In terms of closeness in time, he lived around 400 B.C.E. and may well have been alive when Artaxerxes I died. His history of Persia ceases with the year 398/7 B.C.E. (Diodoros XIV 46,6 [König 1972: 164]). In terms of closeness in place, he lived for a time at the Persian court of Artaxerxes II. In terms of closeness in person, he served as a personal physician to the Persian king Artaxerxes II (405/4 B.C.E.–359/8 B.C.E.).

It is difficult to think of a witness more ideally situated to report on what happened to the Persian royal dynasty in the late fifth century B.C.E., especially if that witness is by all appearance a highly educated and articulate individual. Demetrios of Phaleron (born *ca.* 350 B.C.E.) says about Ktesias that many who may rightly consider him "too garrulous" (ἀδολεσχότερος) fail to appreciate his ἐναργεία, his ability to describe something vividly and palpably (König 1972: 132).

Recently, considerations of the chronological kind pertaining to Artaxerxes I's Babylonian Year 41 have led Zawadzki (1995–96: 48) to conclude that Ktesias' account "does not relate the actual course of events" regarding what happened after Artaxerxes I's death but instead transmits a propagandistic version concocted at the court of Darius II. In other words, Ktesias was enlisted by agents of the Persian court to help spread a biased and inaccurate account of what had happened.

Ktesias' report about the change of rule may be summarized as follows. Artaxerxes I died after having been king for 42 years (§43 end). It is not said where, when, or how, but presumably at Susa in Elam, about 400 kilometers east of Babylon (see below). Zawadzki (1995–96: 47) opens his evaluation of Ktesias' reliability by branding these "42 years" as "proof" of a "mistake." Coming at the beginning of Zawadzki's argument and occurring each only once in it, the words "proof" and "mistake" are loaded terms that seem to set the tone for the rest of his argument. No one in fact assumes that Artaxerxes I reigned longer than 41 years. Then again, it seems clear that Ktesias does not refer to the period in which Artaxerxes I was sole ruler of Persia but rather to the time when he bore the title "king." That explains why he assigns 35 years to the reign of Darius II (§56) when no one doubts that Darius II was absolute ruler for only about 19 years and assigns 18 years to the reign of Cambyses (§12) when Cambyses was absolute ruler for only about 8 years. Clearly, Ktesias' account does not necessarily begin with a "mistake."

Artaxerxes I is succeeded on the day of his death by his only "legitimate" (γνήσιος) son Xerxes (II) and his body along with that of Xerxes' mother Damaspia, who died on the same day, is transported "to Persia" (εἰς Πέρσας). The endpoint of this journey must have been the site of Naqš-i Rustam in Persia located about 500 km to the east close to the capital city of Persepolis in Persia. Both Artaxerxes I and Darius II are presumably buried there, even if definitive evidence is wanting (cf. Briant 2002 [1996]: 170) (§44). Consequently, the beginning point of this long voyage must have been Susa, where Artaxerxes I resided (cf. Nehemiah 1:1, Esther 1:2,5, Daniel 8:2). Exactly 45 days after his father's death, Xerxes II is murdered by a band of conspirators led by Sekyndianos, another son of Artaxerxes I by the Babylonian Alogune. Sekyndianos becomes king but the army hates him (ἐμίσουν αὐτὸν) (§46). Sekyndianos approaches Ochos (Ὦχος), who reluctantly becomes king (§47). At some point, Sekyndianos is emprisoned, "thrown into the ash" (εἰς τὴν σποδὸν ἐμβάλλεται), and dies, having been king (βασιλεύσας) for six months and 15 days (§48). Ochos adopts the name Darius and now rules "alone" (μόνος), suggesting that he and Sekyndianos may have been co-regents earlier (§49). As regards lengths of reign, Diodoros (XII 71,1) and Manetho both give Xerxes II two months and Sekyndianos ("Sogdianos") seven months, for a total of nine together (cf. Kugler 1907–24, vol. 2.2.2: 395).

The transition from Artaxerxes I to Xerxes II appears to have been regular. As Artaxerxes I's only legitimate son, Xerxes II succeeded immediately to the throne. Turmoil erupted when Xerxes was murdered 45 days later. Stability returned with the sole rule of Darius II.

2.2. Three Problems

2.2.1. Main Problem: Winter 425/24 B.C.E. or Winter 424/23 B.C.E.?

Like Alexander's death, Artaxerxes I's a century earlier has generated intense chronological inquiry in modern times. In both cases, the range of uncertainty regarding the date of the event has extended to about a year. In the case of Alexander, this time-span lasts from the late spring or early summer of 324 B.C.E. to about the same time in 323 B.C.E. In the case of Artaxerxes I's death, the year lasts from winter 425/24 B.C.E. to winter 424/23 B.C.E. But this is where the similarity ends. As problems of chronology, the dates of the two events have had different histories. In the case of Alexander's death, the debate has moved decisively from uncertainty to certainty. In the beginning of the nineteenth century, there was still fundamental disagreement about whether he had died at the beginning or the end of the year-long span described above. An investigation by Ludwig Ideler (see §8) once and for all brought the correct time of death, within a range of five days or so, firmly out in front.

In the case of Artaxerxes I's death, the debate has moved decisively from certainty to uncertainty. In Ideler's time, the Greek sources was what one needed to rely on. They left little reason to doubt that Artaxerxes I had died in the winter of 425/24 B.C.E. (see Diodoros XII 64 and Thucydides IV 50 as interpreted, for example, by Meyer 1899: 482–83). The emergence of cuneiform evidence changed all this. In the later nineteenth century, numerous attestations of Artaxerxes I's Year 41 surfaced in contemporary business records. It also became clear that his Babylonian Year 41 had lasted from spring 424 B.C.E. to spring 423 B.C.E. and therefore began after the winter of 425/24 B.C.E. Both Thucydides and the cuneiform record possess sterling reputations as historical sources. About the following there can be no doubt. If taken at face value, either the Greek authors or the Babylonian documents must be wrong.

As a result, there have been various efforts to suggest that either the Greek sources or the Babylonian sources are not what they look like at first sight. Following Kugler, I recently (Depuydt 1995a) suggested that Year 41 of the Babylonian sources is not what it looks like and that Artaxerxes I therefore died in the winter of 425/24 B.C.E. But now, additional cuneiform evidence has come to light. What is more, this evidence has been used to suggest that, to the contrary, it is the Greek sources that are not what they look like (Zawadzki 1995–96). Yet, far from contradicting Kugler's interpretation of Year 41, I believe that the new evidence rather strengthens it. The time seems right to revisit the matter. Not every argument mentioned or every bibliographical reference adduced in the earlier investigation (Depuydt 1995a) will be repeated here.

There are several facets to this problem. The focus will be on one facet, namely that the Babylonian Year 41 has to be a chronological fiction if Artaxerxes I died at the earlier time.

2.2.2. Two Related Problems: Date of Artaxerxes I's Death and Date of Darius II's Accession

Once it has been determined whether Artaxerxes I died in the winter of 425/24 B.C.E. or in the winter of 424/23 B.C.E., the dates of two events can be calibrated: Artaxerxes I's death plus end of reign and Darius II's accession. If Artaxerxes I died in the winter of 425/24 B.C.E., then the first event involves in fact two dates: the end of Artaxerxes I's actual reign at his death and the end of his fictional reign months later.

Owing to the nature of the evidence, a close relationship exists between the main problem and the date of Artaxerxes I's death. The reason is that certain evidence in favor of winter 425/24 B.C.E. over winter 424/23 B.C.E. as the time of Artaxerxes I's death also makes it possible to narrow the time when he most likely died to a 22-day period in early 424 B.C.E.

2.3. Newly Emerged Evidence: Three Cuneiform Tablets

The focus is on new evidence relevant to the three problems in the form of three tablets from Babylon. BM 34684 + 34787 was published by Hunger (2001: 34–38 [no. 9]) and BM 54557 by Zawadzki (1995–96). Bertin 2889 remains unpublished at the time of writing, as far as I know (cf. Bertin 1883).

As regards the relation between the three tablets and the three problems, all three tablets are relevant to the first problem. The two tablets BM 34684 + 34787 and BM 54557 are relevant to the second problem. Only Bertin 2889 adds refinement to the treatment of the third problem. The specific contributions of each tablet to each problem will be detailed below.

2.4. Winter 425/24 B.C.E. or Winter 424/23 B.C.E.?

2.4.1. Long Known Evidence in Favor of Winter 425/24 B.C.E.:
The Greek Sources (Thucydides, Diodoros, and Ktesias)

The Greek sources unanimously support the early alternative as the date of Artaxerxes I's death. The three principal sources are Ktesias, Thucydides, and Diodoros.

Ktesias' account (§2.1) describes in such abundant detail that there was a gap between Artaxerxes I's death and Darius II's accession that the question imposes itself pressingly as to why he would lie. Diodoros (XII 64,1–65,1) clearly places the former's death before the Olympic games, which were held in the summer of 424 B.C.E. Thucydides' report (IV 50) allows moving the death to even earlier. Thucydides places the event not too long before the partial solar eclipse of 21 Mar 424 B.C.E. (IV 52), say in January or February 424 B.C.E.

The manner in which Thucydides reports Artaxerxes I's death exhibits a certain complexity that is in danger of casting doubt on the fact that he placed the event before and not after the eclipse in question. Still, I do not doubt that a paragon of historical reliability like Thucydides believed that Artaxerxes I had died in early 424 B.C.E. (cf. Depuydt 1995a: 87–90).

While recounting events that no doubt happened before the eclipse, Thucydides casts a look into the future and mentions a related event that happened "later" (ὕστερον), it is not said whether before or after the eclipse. Some time "later" Athenian ambassadors sent to Ephesos learn there that Artaxerxes I had "recently" (νεωστί) died. From the future point in time described by the adverb "later," the adverb "recently" casts a look backward into the past. But how far into the past? As a reference to an earlier event, "recently" is vague. But it would appear that Thucydides wants the adverb "recently" to bring his narrative as far back into the past as the adverb "later" has moved it into the future, that is, right back to the point in time before the eclipse at which his main narrative had arrived. Thucydides achieves this by clarifying what "recently" means. He equates "recently" with κατὰ τοῦτον τὸν χρόνον "at this time" by means of the parenthetical statement Κατὰ γὰρ τοῦτον τὸν χρόνον ἐτελεύτησεν "For he died around this time." The use of γὰρ "for" marks this statement as an independent main sentence. This independent main sentence disrupts another independent main statement as follows: οἳ πυθόμενοι αὐτόθι βασιλέα ʼΑρταξέρξην τὸν Ξέρξου νεωστὶ τεθνηκότα (Κατὰ γὰρ τοῦτον τὸν χρόνον ἐτελεύτησεν) ἐπ' οἴκου ἀνεχώρησαν "Learning in that very place that Artaxerxes son of Xerxes had recently died (For he died around this time), they returned home." An independent statement disrupting another independent statement without the two being grammatically linked to one another is conventionally placed between parentheses in English and typically clarifies a certain term in that other statement, in this case "recently." Moreover, the near demonstrative τοῦτον "this" cannot refer to the time when the Athenian ambassadors were in Ephesus because, from their perspective, Artaxerxes I had already died "recently." There is no other point in time to which "this" could refer other than the time shortly before the eclipse where the main narrative has arrived.

2.4.2. Long Known Evidence in Favor of Winter 424/23 B.C.E.: The Babylonian "Year 41"

There is in a sense only one argument in favor of winter 424/23 B.C.E. But its strength cannot be underestimated. It is that cuneiform tablets no doubt kept being dated to the reign of Artaxerxes I until at least late December 424 B.C.E. This undeniable fact stands at the very center of the following discussion.

2.4.3. Artaxerxes I's Babylonian "Year 41"

2.4.3.1. "Year 41": Fact or Fiction?

Artaxerxes I's death cannot have occurred both before the Olympic games as Diodoros states and after them as the cuneiform dates seem to imply. In other words, Artaxerxes I only died in the winter of 425/24 B.C.E. if his Babylonian Year 41 is not what it seems to be at first sight. One explanation would be that scribes kept dating documents according to his reign for months after his death. Such an explanation seems less unusual if one considers that what happened after Artaxerxes I's death was unusual.

Whether the Babylonian Year 41 was real or fictional does not affect the dating of the documents. Everyone without exception equates Year 41—whether it was fictional or factual—with the Babylonian year that lasted from spring 424 B.C.E. to spring 423 B.C.E. And to my knowledge, everyone most always has in the past, with one notable exception, Eduard Meyer (1899: 484–85).

I have elsewhere (Depuydt 1995a: 90–91 with note 12) presented Meyer as the historian who first interpreted the Babylonian Year 41 as fictional. But I failed to add that he did so only for instances of Year 41 in historical and astronomical records. Meyer considered it "unthinkable" (*undenkbar*) that scribes would date business documents to a dead king. He saw only one "way out" (*Ausweg*): business documents were dated a year earlier than dates with the same year date in Babylonian historiography and astronomy.

According to Meyer, two ways of dating years simultaneously prevailed in Babylon. What was, for example, Year 39 of the astronomers and historians was Year 40 of the scribes of business documents. Year 1 of the business documents would then last from spring 465 B.C.E. to spring 464 B.C.E. and Year 41 from spring 425 B.C.E. to spring 424 B.C.E.

This scenario seems highly improbable. I have not found it mentioned anywhere since Meyer proposed it more than a century ago. Meyer's proposal is contradicted by the collective picture derived from all the evidence that has emerged since. But rebutting the proposal here explicitly may not be superfluous. The following counter-argument will need to suffice. Xerxes I's murder is dated in the astronomical record to August 465 B.C.E. in what was his Babylonian Year 21 (see §1). According to Meyer, Artaxerxes I's Year 1 began in business documents already in 465 B.C.E. That would leave no room for an accession year between the end of Xerxes I's reign and the beginning of Artaxerxes I's reign. However, the accession year is now attested in a recently emerged cuneiform business document from Uruk (von Weiher 1998: 123–24 [no. 307]; cf. Stolper 1999: 3). The accession year had already been known from an Aramaic papyrus from Egypt (Porten 1990: 21, "C 6"). Artaxerxes I's accession year therefore lasted until the spring of 464 B.C.E. and his Year 1 began then, not a year earlier in the spring of 465 B.C.E.

The fact remains that Meyer, whose contributions to ancient chronology are unsurpassed, was the first to interpret Year 41 as fictional. But he did not consider it fictional in all cuneiform sources. Kugler was the first who did. And for many decades, he was alone. Until Kugler, most everyone interpreted the Greek sources and cuneiform sources as radically contradicting one another. Kugler was the first to propose that they rather confirm one another.

2.4.3.2. The Return of "Year 41" in Double Dates of Darius II's Accession Year

When Meyer studied Artaxerxes I's Babylonian Year 41, no business documents dating to the accession year of Darius II had come to light (Meyer 1899: 483 bottom). But soon after, Clay (1904, 1908) published a large number of tablets from Nippur. Many of them were written in Darius II's accession year. Clay himself (1904: 16) otherwise believed that Artaxerxes I had died at the end of his Year 41 in the winter of 424/23 B.C.E. But Kugler took a closer look at the Nippur tablets and reached a different conclusion.

Kugler (1907-24: 395-97) accepted that the Greek sources left little doubt that Artaxerxes I had died in early 424 B.C.E. But as an Assyriologist, he knew as well as anyone that the dates of cuneiform business documents have a sterling reputation for historical reliability. It is in this connection that he made a crucial empirical observation regarding the Nippur tablets that led him to the conclusion that the cuneiform evidence and the Greek evidence mutually confirmed one another. He took note of the fact—as others surely did before him without making anything of it—that the tablets dating to Darius II's accession year contain two different formulas denoting the year. The first is single and refers to the year simply as "Accession Year of Darius (II)." The second is double and refers to the year as "Year 41 (of Artaxerxes I), Accession Year of Darius (II)."

What Kugler then observed was that *all the single dates as a rule precede all the double dates* (for the details, see below). The following periods can therefore be distinguished in the dating of documents:

> dating by Year 40 of Artaxerxes (I);
> dating by Year 41 of Artaxerxes (I);
> dating by Accession Year of Darius (II);
> dating by Year 41, Accession Year of Darius (II).

It appeared to him that this peculiar empirical fact could be explained as confirming that Artaxerxes I had died a year earlier. Kugler's explanation failed to gain attention, let alone acceptance. Perhaps the reason is that it was buried deep in his highly technical *Sternkunde und Sterndienst in Babel* (1907-24). As a result, Artaxerxes I's death has in recent decades typically been dated to winter 424/23 B.C.E. After reviewing the evidence that came to light in the seventy years since Kugler's publication (Depuydt 1995a), it seemed to me that his explanation had held up rather well against the evidence. New evidence could conceivably have contradicted it. But it has not. Future evidence still might.

What is remarkable about the dating formula "Year 41, Accession Year of Darius" is not that it is double or that "Year 41" is used after Artaxerxes I's reign had ended, but rather the return of "Year 41" after an absence of a couple of months. In fact, other double dates are known, including from the ends of the reigns of both Artaxerxes I's predecessor Xerxes I and his successor Darius II. "Year 21 (of Xerxes I), Accession Year of Artaxerxes (I)" occurs in a tablet from Uruk (see §1 end). "Year 19 (of Darius II), Accession Year of Artaxerxes (II)" is preserved in a tablet from Babylon (§3). "Year 2 (of Arses), Accession Year of Darius (III)" appears in an Aramaic papyrus from Wadi Daliyeh (see §6).

Reacting to my assessment of Kugler's theory in a postscript to his publication of BM 54557, Zawadzki (1995-96: 49) laconically declares that evidence derived from BM 54557 makes dating Artaxerxes I's death to the end of his Year 40 in early 424 B.C.E. "unacceptable." But he does not elaborate, presumably because the remark needed to be added hastily in a postscript. In fact, Kugler's proposal is mentioned neither in the article nor in the postscript. Briant (2001: 90 with note 160) cites Zawadzki's verdict of "unacceptable," but without further comment. I have the impression, however, that BM 54557 does not at all disprove that Artaxerxes I died in his Year 40. If anything, it strengthens Kugler's proposal.

No one is right all the time and authority should never count for anything. What is more, future evidence may still contradict Kugler's theory. Still, students of chronology should relish any opportunity to rally to the defense of a view of Kugler's. Few have contributed as much to ancient chronology. His *Babylonische*

Mondrechnung (1900) is one of the great intellectual feats of the twentieth century in Assyriology if not in any field of the humanities.

2.4.3.3. Kugler's Interpretation of the Return of "Year 41" as Evidence in Favor of 425/24 B.C.E.

What happened in the dating of cuneiform documents in 424–23 B.C.E. if one is to believe Kugler? Artaxerxes I died near the end of his Year 40 in early 424 B.C.E. His son Xerxes II succeeded him but was murdered after 45 days. Scribes kept dating cuneiform documents fictionally to Artaxerxes I's reign. Artaxerxes I must therefore already have been dead when an eclipse text dated to Month 13 (second Addaru) of his Year 40 was inscribed on tablet BM 36910 + 36998 + 37036 (*PD* 9). At the Babylonian new year in the spring, Artaxerxes I's fictional Year 41 began. Scribes kept dating documents by this year until at least Month 9 Day 12, that is, *ca.* 24 Dec 424 B.C.E. (*PD* 18), the date of the latest known instance. But by Month 9 Day 29, that is, *ca.* 10 Jan 423 B.C.E., which is the date of BM 54557 (Zawadzki 1995–96), fictional dating ceased and scribes began dating by Darius II's accession year. They did so for some weeks, when pure actual dating ended and fictional dating partly returned in the form of the dating formula "Year 41, Accession Year of Darius (II)." The earliest instance of this dating formula is dated to Month 11 Day 26 found in the unpublished tablet Bertin 2889. Artaxerxes I is not mentioned in this formula. "Accession Year of Darius II" is actual. But "Year 41" is fictional because the reigns of the two kings did not overlap. Together "Year 41 (of Artaxerxes I)" and "Accession Year of Darius (II)" make up the full Babylonian year that lasted from spring 424 B.C.E. to spring 423 B.C.E. "Year 41, Accession Year of Darius II" could therefore be interpreted as a way of describing the entire span of that Babylonian calendar year. On new year or Month 1 Day 1 or Nisanu 1 in the spring of 423 B.C.E., that is, *ca.* 11 April, Darius II's Babylonian Year 1 began.

Kugler inferred from said return of "Year 41" in documents from Darius II's accession year that Artaxerxes I had died a year earlier. For clarity's sake, the manner in which this inference is drawn may be articulated in a number of cumulative steps.

Step one: Uniqueness of the Return of "Year 41."—The return of "Year 41" is unique in its kind. Its uniqueness raises the question as to what else was unique about the transition between the two reigns.

Step two: Unique Character of the Transition.—The Greek sources leave little doubt that the transition from Artaxerxes I to Darius II was different in nature from other transitions in indicating that Artaxerxes I's death and Darius II's accession were separated by an interval of time. The question arises if the unique interval and the unique return of "Year 41" can be related to one another. But first, one kind of interval needs to be eliminated from consideration because its length is not certain.

Step three: Length of Interval between Reigns Uncertain and therefore Unusable.—The length of the interval from Artaxerxes I's death to Darius II's accession is not exactly known from the Greek sources. Above all, an overlap of Sekyndianos' and Darius II's reigns would shorten this interval. But it seems the interval needs to be counted, not in weeks or years, but in months. Lengths of eight to nine months can be inferred from the Greek sources and Ktesias reports enough events to fill that many months (§2.1). There is another interval, however, beginning with Artaxerxes I's death whose length can be measured more precisely using the Greek sources.

Step four: Interval between Death and Return of "Year 41" about a Year Long.—The interval from Artaxerxes I's death to the return of "Year 41" in dating formulas happens to be about a year long. Thucydides dates the death to about February 424 B.C.E. The return of "Year 41" dates to about the same time of year one year later in 423 B.C.E. The question arises whether the return of "Year 41" and the fact that it happened about a year after the death of Artaxerxes I can be linked to one another. In trying to answer this question, it is useful to consider the notion that something might reappear because its absence would be misleading. The question may therefore be rephrased as follows: What kind of confusion might the absence of "Year 41" cause in relation to the death of Artaxerxes I a year earlier?

Step five: Possible Confusion in the Absence of "Year 41."—The return of "Year 41" seems to entertain a relation with Artaxerxes I's death. How could the absence of "Year 41" be misleading? In theory at least, the answer to this question is obvious. In the absence of "Year 41," a scribe years later consulting both historical and business records could encounter two items of information.

The historical record would show that Artaxerxes I had died on Month x Day x at the end of his Year 40. The business record would contain documents dated to a month and day date in the accession year of Darius II that falls later in the calendar year than the month and day date of Artaxerxes I's death. Nothing in this information would prevent a scribe from concluding that Darius II had succeeded Artaxerxes I at the end of his Year 40, a year before he actually did. The omission of a year might affect and confuse financial transactions and all kinds of business agreements.

Two items of information that could have averted the above conclusion would be wanting from both records, namely traces of the reigns of Xerxes II or Sekyndianos or an explicit statement that scribes kept dating documents by Artaxerxes I's reign after his death. In the absence of these two items of information, the presence of another item could prevent confusion.

Step six: Adding "Year 41" to Avoid Confusion.—Adding "Year 41" to month and day dates in the "Accession Year of Darius (II)" falling after the month and day date of Artaxerxes I's death makes it impossible to place the document at the end of Year 40.

2.4.3.4. The Evidence for Kugler's Interpretation of the Return of "Year 41":
Posteriority of the Double Dates

Kugler's interpretation of "Year 41" serves as an argument in favor of winter 425/24 B.C.E. as the time of death of Artaxerxes I. But what evidence supports the interpretation itself? The principal argument has always been that all instances of the single date "Accession Year of Darius (II)" precede all instances of the double date "Year 41 (of Artaxerxes I), Accession Year of Darius (II)." It was on the basis of this fact that Kugler advanced his interpretation in the first place. According to the evidence accessible in Kugler's time, *three* double dates followed *three* single dates in time. In an update of the evidence seventy years after the time when Kugler made his proposal (Depuydt 1995a), the posteriority of all the double dates was upheld and *five* double dates now followed *four* single dates. The two newly accessible tablets BM 54557 and Bertin 2889 can now be added to the evidence. As a result, *five* double dates now follow *five* single dates. The evidence as it now stands is surveyed below. In serving as evidence of Kugler's interpretation of the return of "Year 41" in dating formulas of Darius II's accession year, BM 54557 and Bertin 2889 also indirectly serve as evidence of winter 425/24 B.C.E. as the time of Artaxerxes I's death. Furthermore, Bertin 2889 will be adduced below as new evidence for calibrating the date of Artaxerxes I's death more precisely and BM 54557 will be adduced as new evidence for calibrating the date of Darius II's accession more precisely.

As it now stands, the evidence consists of eleven tablets. They are listed with details below. Nos. 2, 4, 5, 8, 9, and 10 were known to Kugler. Nos. 3, 7, and 11 were added in a recent update (Depuydt 1995a). Nos. 1 and 6 are added presently. The tablets are listed below in two columns, one for tablets from Babylon and one for tablets from Nippur. The abbreviations *Kug*, *Dep*, and *new* indicate when a tablet was first adduced as evidence. For the special case of no. 9 in the following list, see §2.4.3.5 below.

Kug = First adduced in Kugler 1907–24, vol. 2.2.2: 395–97.
Dep = First adduced in Depuydt 1995a.
new = Newly adduced here.

MONTH AND DAY DATE		BABYLON	NIPPUR	
Dated to "Accession Year of Darius II" (single date)				
(1)	Month 9 Day 29	*new* BM 54557		
(2)	Month 11 Day 4	*Kug* BE X no. 1		
(3)	Month 11 Day 14		*Dep*	Ni(ppur) 2668
(4)	Month 11 Day 15		*Kug*	BE X no. 2
(5)	Month 11 Day 15		*Kug*	BE X no. 3
Dated to "Year 41, Accession Year of Darius II" (double date)				
(6)	Month 11 Day 26	*new* Bertin 2889		
(7)	Month 11 Day 29	*Dep* BM 33342		
(8)	Month 12 Day 14		*Kug*	BE X no. 4
?(9)	[Month 12 Day 17		Kug	BE X no. 5]
(10)	Month 12 Day 20		*Kug*	BE VIII.1 no. 127
(11)	Month 12 Day 22		*Dep*	PBS II.1 no. 1

All tablets except Bertin 2889 (cf. Bertin 1883) are published, as follows.

	TABLET	PUBLICATION
(1)	BM 54557	Zawadzki 1995–96
(2)	BE X no. 1	Clay 1904
(3)	Ni 2668	Donbaz and Stolper 1997: 99–100 (no. 23)
(4)	BE X no. 2	Clay 1904
(5)	BE X no. 3	Clay 1904
(6)	Bertin 2889	unpublished (cf. Bertin 1883)
(7)	BM 33342	Stolper 1983: 231–36
(8)	BE X no. 4	Clay 1904
(9)	BE X no. 5	Clay 1904
(10)	BE VIII.1 no. 127	Clay 1908
(11)	PBS II.1 no. 1	Clay 1912

The new tablet BM 54557 contains three dates, of which the first two are connected, as follows:

(line 4)	ITI.NE	MU.41.KÁM	$^{p}Ár$-[tak-šat-su]
	"(from)Abu (Month 5),	Year 41	of Artaxerxes";
(lines 5–6)	ITI.ŠE	MU.41.[KÁM] | MU.SAG	^{p}Da-ri-ja-muš
	"(until) Addaru (Month 12),	Year 41, Accession Year	of Darius";
(line 21)	ITI.GAN U$_4$.29.KÁM	MU.SAG	^{p}Da-r[i-ja-muš]
	"Kislimu (Month 9), Day 29,	Accession Year	of Darius."

The document was written on Month 9 Day 29. The scribe adds "Year 41" to the reference to Month 12 of Darius II's accession year in lines 5–6. By contrast, "Year 41" is *not* added to the reference to Month 12 in the formula "from Month 1 of Year 41 to the end of Month 12 of the Accession Year of Darius (II)" in tablet *BE* X no. 6 (Clay 1904). A possible explanation is as follows. In thinking of Month 12 or the end the calendar year, the entire calendar year may come to mind and therefore also the fact that the year had consisted of two portions belonging to two reigns. The scribe of BM 54557 made this fact explicit. The scribe of *BE* X no. 6 did not.

2.4.3.5. *BE* X no. 5 as a Weak Link in Kugler's Interpretation of "Year 41"'s Return

Tablet *BE* X no. 5 is placed between square brackets in italics in the table in §2.4.3.4 to call attention to its special status. Kugler (1907–24, vol. 2.2.2: 396) had already observed that it is an exception to the rule in that it contains a *single* date that falls later than certain *double* dates. By theory, one expects all the single dates to predate all the double dates. However, line 1 of *BE* X no. 5 contains the expression "until the end of Addaru of Year 41, Accession Year of Darius (II)." Kugler therefore assumed that, since Month 12 (Addaru) had already been associated with Year 41 in line 1, the scribe deemed it superfluous to associate Month 12 again with Year 41 later in the text. This assumption makes the single date of *BE* X no. 5 into a truncated double date. This is why it has been classified with the double dates and not with the single dates in the list in §2.4.3.4 above, even though it is at first sight a single date.

Still, *BE* X no. 5 does weaken Kugler's explanation of the return of "Year 41." But discarding the explanation seems premature, like throwing out the baby with the bath water. A number of considerations compensate for the weakening effect of *BE* X no. 5.

First, not every scribe may have applied "Year 41" rigorously. Its application implies a sophisticated understanding of how a dating formula can lead to confusion in light of the unique historical circumstances of 424–23 B.C.E.

Second, a *double* date *preceding* the *latest single* date is much more damaging to Kugler's interpretation than a *single* date *following* the *earliest double* date. A convention can always be continued out of sheer habit. But a convention cannot be applied before there is reason for it to exist. Likewise, iron tools could hardly predate the Iron Age.

Third, the scribe of *BE* X no. 5 five days later wrote *PBS* II.1 no. 1, in which he does use a double date as Kugler's interpretation requires (cf. Depuydt 1995a: 94 note 33). Perhaps, he had learned a thing or two.

Fourth, in the list of tablets in §2.4.3.4, five single dates still precede five double dates without *BE* X no. 5.

Fifth, in the city of Babylon, the intellectual capital of the empire, Kugler's scheme still holds up %100. Two tablets with single dates precede two tablets with double dates.

If the single date involving Month 12 in *BE* X no. 5 is a truncated double date as Kugler assumes, then why would the single date involving Month 9 in BM 54557 (see §2.4.3.4) not also be a truncated double date? After all, in both tablets, "Year 41" has been mentioned earlier in the text. Both absences of "Year 41" could therefore be interpreted as non-repetitions and in that sense not really as absences. There is a difference, however, between *BE* X no. 5 and BM 54557. In *BE* X no. 5, the earlier mention of "Year 41" accompanies the same Month 12. It is therefore slightly easier to interpret "Month 12" as an abbreviation of the earlier mentioned "Month 12, Year 41." But in BM 54557, the earlier mention of "Year 41" involves a different month, namely Month 5. It is therefore not possible to interpret "Month 9" as an abbreviation of an earlier mentioned "Month 5, Year 41."

2.4.4. New Cuneiform Evidence in Favor of Winter 425/24 B.C.E.:
Artaxerxes I Died before the Total Eclipse of 4 Apr 424 B.C.E. according to BM 34684 + 34787

The assumption has been widespread that the Greek sources point to the winter of 425/24 B.C.E. as the time when Artaxerxes I died whereas the cuneiform sources rather suggest winter 424/23 B.C.E. Accordingly, there has been a certain tendency for classicists to defend the earlier date and Assyriologists the later date. It fell to an Assyriologist, Kugler, to propose that the cuneiform sources support the Greek sources in favor of the earlier date. Kugler's proposal has been discussed in detail above. It is now possible to adduce a new piece of cuneiform evidence that also supports the early date and goes a long way towards cementing the veracity of the Greek sources and of Kugler's hypothesis of the return of "Year 41" at some point in Darius II's accession year.

The new evidence concerns the description of transitions of reign in astronomical texts. Before the beginning of the Seleucid Era in 311 B.C.E., the counting of years began anew with every new reign. Exact dating is of capital importance in astronomy. Distances in time between two celestial events that are years if not centuries apart need to be measured with absolute precision. An error of one day or even just one hour would render any further computations useless.

One facet of dating is the turning points that come at the ends of reigns, when the counting of the years starts over again. In Babylon, the end of a reign is not followed by Year 1 of the next reign but by a period called the accession year (MU.SAG). Year 1 begins with the first New Year's Day of the reign. The scribes of astronomical texts took care to mention the end of the reign along with a brief description of what happened. As Walker observes (1997: 21), "the [astronomical] tablets apparently gave details, at the appropriate points, of the death of the reigning king."

In this respect, a most striking fact emerges. The end of Artaxerxes I's reign is left unmentioned where one expects it, in sharp contrast with what is transmitted about the other ends of reigns. Not only can it be inferred from the text that nothing happened to Artaxerxes I shortly before Darius ascended to the throne at the very end of 424 B.C.E. or the very beginning of 423 B.C.E.—presumably because he had died months earlier—but also that his actual reign ended before the total eclipse of 4 Apr 424 B.C.E., that is, Babylonian Month 13 (second Addaru) Day 14 or, less likely, Day 15. The eclipse was not visible at Babylon, Susa, or Persepolis. But it definitely was further east in the Achaemenid empire.

It will be useful to gather all that is said about transitions of reigns before 311 B.C.E. in Babylonian astronomical records, from when they first begin in 747 B.C.E., in a period of a little more than four centuries. There is no doubt that a continuous record once existed for every month in this period. But much of this record has been lost. The farther one recedes into the past, the more fragmentary the record becomes.

Only little remains of the record for the first two to three centuries. In fact, before the mention of Xerxes I's murder (465), none of the preserved and published astronomical tablets pertain to the transition of a reign, as far as I know. Yet, one assumes that the death of each king and the accession of his successor must have been mentioned, along with the briefest of indications of the circumstances in which the kingship changed hands. One assumes that the historical record also details all the transitions. References to the accession of Nabopolassar (626) and his death (Month 5 Day 21 in 605), the accession of Nebuchadrezzar (Month 6 Day 1 of 605), and the entrance of Cyrus into Babylon Month 8 (Day 3 of 539) have survived in the Babylonian Chronicle (*PD* 11–13).

From Xerxes I onward, a remarkably high number of the transitions of reign have been preserved entirely or in fragments. As was noted above, twelve main transitions occurred in the Achaemenid empire. The present paper present updates on the chronology of the last nine of them (§§1–9). References or fragments of references to seven of these nine transitions, about 78%, survive. These seven transitions are the following:

(1) Xerxes I	to Artaxerxes I	(465)	see §1
(2) Artaxerxes I	to Darius II	(424–23)	see §2
(4) Artaxerxes II	to Artaxerxes III	(359/58)	see §4
(5) Artaxerxes III	to Arses	(338)	see §5
(7) Darius III	to Alexander III	(331)	see §7
(8) Alexander III	to Philip Arridaios	(323)	see §8
(9) Philip Arridaios	to Alexander IV	(317)	see §9

No preserved and published astronomical tablets concern the following two transitions, as far as I know:

(3) Darius II	to Artaxerxes II	(405/4)	see §3
(6) Arses	to Darius III	(336/35)	see §6

References to five of the seven transitions listed above are preserved in eclipse texts (Hunger 2001). References to two transitions, namely Darius III to Alexander III (331) and Alexander III to Philip Arridaios (323), survive in the Diaries (Sachs and Hunger 1988). In one of these two, the transition from Darius III to Alexander III, the end of reign is not a king's death but Darius III's defeat at the battle of Gaugamela (331). Alexander's entry into Babylon followed soon after. The full text of the references to the seven transitions is as follows.

REFERENCES TO ACHAEMENID REGNAL TRANSITIONS
IN BABYLONIAN ASTRONOMICAL TEXTS

(1) Xerxes I to Artaxerxes I (465):

BM 32234 (Hunger 2001: 20–21 [no. 4])

Rev.´ IV´

    4´   Month 5, Day 14$^?$, Xerxes, his son killed him.

(2) Artaxerxes I to Darius II (424–23):

BM 34684 + 34787 (Hunger 2001: 36–37 [no. 9])

Rev.´ II´

    1´   [....] ....

    2´   [....] was seen. [....]

    3´   [....] was eclipsed. Jupiter was in Sagittarius, Saturn was [....] behind β Capricorni [....]

    4´   [(Year) 41], Month 6, Day 14$^?$, 50°$^?$ after sunset, it began in the east and north. In 22° it left 2 fingers remaining to totality. 5° maximal phase. In 23° [it cleared] to [....]

    5´   [....] 50° onset, maximal phase, and clearing. The "garment of the sky" was there, the west wind blew. 3 cubits below α + β Arietis [it was eclipsed.]

    6´   Accession year of Umakuš (Ochos), who is called$^?$ Darius [...]

    7´   (Year) 1, Month 5 (*and so on*)

(4) Artaxerxes II to Artaxerxes III (Ochos) (359/58):

BM 71537 (Hunger 2001: 42–43 [no. 11])

II´ Obv.

    1´   [....] sat on the throne.

    2´   [Month 11, Day 2]8, ..., omitted.

    3´–4´ (*blank*)

    5´   Year 1 of Umakuš (Ochos) (*and so on*)

(5) Artaxerxes III (Ochos) to Arses (338):

BM 71537 (Hunger 2001: 42, 45 [no. 11])

III´ Rev.

    8   (Year) 21, Month 4, (after) 5 months, Day 29, ..., omitted.

9   Month 6, Umakuš (Ochos) died.

10   Aršu (Arses), his son, sat on the throne.

(7) Darius III to Alexander III (331):

BM 36761 (Sachs and Hunger 1988: 178-79 [no. -330])

´Obv.´

14´   That month, on Day 11, panic occurred in the camp before the king [....]

15´   lay? opposite the king. On Day 24, in the morning, the king of the world [....] the standard? [....]

16´   they fought with each other, and a heavy? defeat of the troops of [....]

17´   the troops of the king deserted him and [went?] to their cities [....]

18´   they fled to the land of the Guti [....]

19´   [Month 7, Day 1 .....]
(*more text*)

´Rev.´

(*more text*)

6´   On Day 11, in Sippar an order of Al[exander ....]

7´   ["...] I shall not enter your houses." On Day 13, [....]

8´   [....] to? the outer gate of Esangila and [....]

9´   [....] On Day 14, these? Ionians a bull [....]

10´   short, fatty tissue [....]

11´   [....] Alexander, king of the world, [came? in]to Babylon [....]

(8) Alexander III to Philip Arridaios (323):

BM 45962 (Sachs and Hunger 1988: 206-7 [no. -322])

´Obv.´

8´   [....] stood [to] the east. Day 29, the king died; clouds [....]

(9) Philip Arridaios to Alexander IV (317):

BM 32238 (Hunger 2001: 6-7 [no. 2])

Rev.´ V´

12´   Month 9, Day 27, Pill[i-....] (Philip Arridaios)

13´   Year 2 of Antigonos

In five of these seven transitions, namely (1), (5), (7), (8), and (9), the end of the reign is explicitly mentioned. In one transition, (1), the end is a murder. In two others, (5) and (8), it is a death. In a fourth, (7), a defeat in battle marks the end. In a fifth, (9), it is not known how the end came because the text is fragmentary. But enough has been preserved of the text to make it plausible that some kind of end is being referred to.

The text of a sixth transition, namely (4), probably contained a reference to the end of Artaxerxes II's reign, but the text is fragmentary. However, transition (4) is mentioned on the same tablet as transition (5). The references to the beginnings of the reigns of Artaxerxes III and Arses are formulated in the same way in both (4) and (5), namely by means of the expression *ina* AŠ-TE TUŠ-*ab* "he sat on the throne." It is therefore quite possible that the references to the ends of the reigns of Artaxerxes II and Artaxerxes III were also formulated similarly and that the text did mention Artaxerxes II's death or whatever way it was in which his reign ended. Briant (2002 [1996]: 681) studied the collective sources of this transition and concludes that "everything leads us to believe that, when Artaxerxes II died, everything was ready for the transition." Moreover, he writes, Diodoros (xv 93,1) "simply notes that, when Artaxerxes II died, Ochos succeeded his father." That leaves only transition (2), which is discussed in more detail below.

For five of the seven transitions, dates have been preserved for the end of the reign. In four cases, (1), (7), (8), and (9), the end of the reign is dated to the exact day; in one case, (5), to the exact month.

In two cases, (7) and (9), the old and new kings are both mentioned in quick succession; in (9), Arridaios' successor Antigonos is mentioned in the date of the next line. In (1), the "son" who killed Xerxes I is perhaps not his successor. In (5), both kings may have been mentioned as well, but the reference to the earlier king is presumably lost.

In (8), the reference to the later king is lost, but Arridaios must have been mentioned very soon after Alexander's death. Tablet BM 34075 (Hunger 2001: 90-91 [no. 36]) begins with the first day of Arridaios' reign, which is the day immediately following the day of death of Alexander, Month 3 Day 1 of his Year 1. The accession year was abandoned from Arridaios onward.

The following pattern emerges. In all probability, in six of the seven reports on transitions of reign, the end of the reign was—or at least must have been—specified and followed by a reference to the beginning of the next reign. Four of these six reports survive in eclipse texts, the type of text in which transition (2) is preserved.

Transition (2), Artaxerxes I to Darius II (424–23), stands out as a unique exception by the absence of any reference to the end of a reign where one expects it in the astronomical record, namely right before the mention of the beginning of the next reign, Darius II's.

The absence occurs in an eclipse text. Babylonian astronomical texts exhibit unsurpassed parsimony and rigor, stating exactly as much as needs be, nothing more, nothing less. Absences are significant. For example, a day number preceded by GE_6 denotes nighttime. In the absence of any marker, the day number refers to daylight.

In light of all else that we know, it is difficult to accept that the astronomical record would have been totally silent about the end of Artaxerxes I's reign. Some reference to the end of his reign must have occurred in the text. The reference to the beginning of Darius II's reign is preceded by the descriptions of two eclipses. The text is continuously preserved from the mention of the first of these two eclipses to the mention of Darius II's accession year (see the text under [2] above). Therefore, the reference to Artaxerxes I, if there was one, could not have been placed later in the text than right before the mention of the first of the two eclipses. Accordingly, his death must be dated at the latest to before the first eclipse.

The second and later eclipse is beyond a doubt the one of 28 Sep 424 B.C.E. (Steele in Hunger 2001: 397). As regards the first eclipse, eclipse possibilities occur at distances of five or six months according to a distinct pattern (see ibid.: 390-91). By the mere inner logic of the text, there is no doubt that the very fragmentary text preceding the reference to the eclipse of 28 Sep 424 B.C.E. must refer to an eclipse possibility six and not five months earlier. That is because an interval of five months between the eclipse of

27 Mar 423 B.C.E. and 20 Aug 423 B.C.E. follows soon after. Intervals of five months are preceded by groups of seven or eight successive intervals of six months. What must be meant by

1´ [....] ....
2´ [....] was seen. [....]
3´ [....] was eclipsed. Jupiter was in Sagittarius, Saturn was [....] behind β Capricorni [....]

in BM 34684 + 34787 (Hunger 2001: 36–37 [no. 9]), at Rev.´ II´, is therefore the eclipse possibility of Month 13 (DIR ŠE or second Addaru) of Year 40 mentioned in the Saros Cycle text preserved in BM 36910 + 36998 + 37036 (Aaboe and others 1991: 4–8; cf. *PD* 9). The reference cannot be but to the total eclipse of 4 Apr 424 B.C.E. Jupiter and Saturn seem to have been closer to the positions stated in the text in 425 B.C.E. Still, in April 424 B.C.E., Saturn was also in Capricorn and Jupiter not far from it in Capricorn towards Sagittarius, still strikingly close to the positions stated in the text. Jupiter had just come from Sagittarius. It also needs to be remembered that the modern zodiac signs do not fully coincide with the Babylonian ones. But I have not further examined the relevance of this fact. Steele (in Hunger 2001: 397) does not identify the eclipse in his list of identifiable eclipses mentioned in the cuneiform eclipse texts published by Hunger.

The eclipse was total and hence a striking phenomenon. It is true that it was not visible in the regions around the capital cities of Babylon (around 44° longitude), Susa (around 48°), and Persepolis (around 53°). Whereas lunar eclipses (as opposed to solar eclipses) have the same appearance everywhere on earth, they are only visible at night (just as solar eclipses are obviously only visible when the sun is). It is otherwise true that the moon can sometimes be seen together with the sun in the sky. However, lunar eclipses occur around full moon when the moon is exactly opposite the sun and therefore below the horizon when the sun is above it.

On the other hand, the eclipse at hand *was* visible eastward from around 60° longitude onward (see www.sunearth.gsfc.nasa.gov/eclipse, a website run by Fred Espenak). The Achaemenid empire extended to about 70° and a little beyond at the time. Accordingly, the eclipse must have been seen in a large area spanning 10° longitudinally and including ancient Bactria and Sogdiana as well as modern easternmost Iran, Afghanistan, and western Pakistan.

Only a few words survive of the description of the eclipse. And yet, it can be argued that the very little that does survive indicates that the report concerns a sighting *outside* Babylon. This argumentation is as follows.

In the previous column on the same side of the same tablet, BM 34684 + 34787, at Rev.´ I´ 3´, the following is stated about an earlier eclipse, the one of 25 Mar 442 B.C.E.:

ina ^{uru}*Šu-šá-an u* EDIN IGI "It was seen in Susa and the open country."

The same IGI "was seen," preceded by a lacuna, is used to describe the eclipse of 4 Apr 424 B.C.E. in a line all of its own in BM 34684 + 34787, at Rev. ´II´ 2´. It seems safe to conclude that IGI "was seen" was used for the same reason as earlier in the same tablet and that the lacuna therefore contained a geographical reference, perhaps EDIN "open country" if EDIN could include the vast stretches of land extending east of Persepolis and also belonging to the empire. Not a single word or sign is used lightly in Babylonian cuneiform texts. "The terminology used in the diaries," write Sachs and Hunger (1988: 38), "is rigid and very condensed. The order of items recorded is also to a large extent fixed. Because of the repetitive character of these texts, the scribes apparently tried to reduce as much as possible the number of words they had to write."

In conclusion, there is a distinct possibility that the end of Artaxerxes I's reign was mentioned in the lost portions of BM 34684 + 34787, presumably near the end of column I´ of the Reverse, because Rev.´ II´ 1´–3´ are "overflow from column I´" (Hunger 2001: 39). Consequently, the presence of certain information and the absence or loss of other information in BM 34684 + 34787 serves as an argument that Artaxerxes I died before 4 Apr 424 B.C.E. Thucydides (IV 50) places the same event not too long before the partial solar eclipse that occurred at the beginning of the same lunar month on 21 Mar 424 B.C.E. (IV 52).

At the very least, the absence of any reference to Artaxerxes I in the text is exceptional and signifies that the transition of reign was unusual.

According to Walker (1997: 22), a "link [was] seen in antiquity between eclipses and the death of kings." This link may not only be magical or religious in purport but also calendrical. Lunar calendars differed from nation to nation in terms of order and lengths of lunar months. But eclipses did not. That may be why they served as chronological anchors in the writings of Thucydides and many other historians.

2.5. The Date of Artaxerxes I's Death: A Day in *ca.* 26 Jan–*ca.* 16 Feb 424 B.C.E.

So far, the discussion has focused on determining whether Artaxerxes I died in the winter of 425/24 B.C.E. or of 424/23 B.C.E. The former date has been defended above. Two newly emerged cuneiform tablets have already been adduced as evidence in favor of winter 425/24 B.C.E. Bertin 2889 and BM 54557 make their own small contribution to the notion that the return of "Year 41" in dating formulas of Darius II's accession year points to winter 425/24 B.C.E. as the sought time (§2.4.3). Tablets BM 34684 + 34787 provided a *terminus ante quem* that places the death several months before winter 424/23 B.C.E. (§2.4.4).

It now remains to be determined to which extent additional calibration of the date is possible. But first, the danger of using evidence of mixed provenance should be highlighted. News pertaining to a transition of reign may arrive at different times in different places. A choice will impose itself. That choice will be Babylon as premier city of the empire. Some decades ago, there was little choice but to use evidence from Nippur because most of the relevant tablets known at the time came from that city. The emergence of tablets BM 54557 and Bertin 2889 from Babylon now allows a decisive shift from Nippur to Babylon.

The danger of using evidence from Nippur and mixing it with evidence of different provenance is obvious from the case of tablet *BE* X no. 109 from Ḫašbâ. The town of Ḫašbâ was probably located near Nippur (Kugler 1907–24, vol. 2.2.2: 389; *PD* 18; Depuydt 1995a: 18 [with references]; id. 1995b: 159 note 28). Tablet *BE* X no. 109 is dated to Month 11 Day 17 of Year 41 of Artaxerxes I, or *ca.* 26 Feb 423 B.C.E. No one—and that includes those who refuse to accept that Year 41 was fictional—now thinks that Artaxerxes I was still alive as late as Month 11 Day 17 of his Year 41. Clay (1904: 2), the editor of the tablet, therefore already assumed an error in the date. Kugler (1907–24, vol. 2.2.2: 389), whose comment I earlier (Depuydt 1995a: 90) overlooked, believed that assuming an error was "a little forced" (*etwas gezwungen*). He proposed instead that the news of Darius II's accession and of the end of Artaxerxes I's reign—regardless of whether that reign was still actual or already fictional—had not yet reached the small town of Ḫašbâ from nearby Nippur. In Kugler's time, the earliest known date of Darius II's accession year from Nippur was still Month 11 Day 15, or *ca.* 13 Feb 423 B.C.E., found in *BE* X no. 2; it now is Month 11 Day 14 in Ni 2668 (§2.4.3.4). According to Ni 2668, Artaxerxes I's reign *could* have been recognized as late as Month 11 Day 13 (Day 14 in Kugler's time, before the emergence of Ni 2668) in Nippur. According to *BE* X no. 109, Artaxerxes I's reign was still recognized as late as Month 11 Day 17 in nearby Ḫašbâ. According to Kugler (cf. *PD* 18), if Artaxerxes I's reign could have ended as late as Day 14 (now Day 13) at the city of Nippur, then it could easily have ended at the nearby little town of Ḫašbâ a few days later because the news of the change of reign was delayed. The earliest date of Darius II's accession from Nippur is now Day 14. At Ḫašbâ, Darius II would then have been recognized from as early as Day 18.

In Kugler's time, the earliest known date belonging to Darius II's accession year from Babylon was Month 11 Day 4, or *ca.* 13 Feb 423 B.C.E., found in *BE* X no. 1. The distance in time between *BE* X no. 1 and *BE* X no. 109 is greater than that between *BE* no. 2 and *BE* X no. 109, suggesting a greater delay in the arrival of news. The geographical distance between Babylon and Ḫašbâ is indeed greater than that between Nippur and Ḫašbâ.

I suggested elsewhere (1995a: 90) that, if it took two weeks or more for the news of Darius II's accession to reach Ḥašbâ from Babylon, then Darius II's accession was probably recognized in Babylon not much earlier than *ca.* 13 Feb 423 B.C.E. The new evidence from BM 54557 (Zawadzki 1995-96) falsifies this suggestion. According to this tablet, Darius II was recognized at Babylon as early as Month 9 Day 29, that is, *ca.* 10 Jan 423 B.C.E. Still, the suggestion might be salvaged if it is modified and *two* delays are assumed, a first from Babylon to Nippur and a second from Nippur to Ḥašbâ. Artaxerxes I *could* have been recognized at Babylon as late as Month 9 Day 28 and at Nippur as late as Month 11 Day 13. At nearby Ḥašbâ, he was recognized until at least four days later, Month 11 Day 17. These observations can be reconciled if one assumes that news of the end of Artaxerxes I's reign reached Nippur from Babylon with a delay of a couple of weeks to up to a month and then Ḥašbâ from Nippur with an additional delay of a few days to up to a couple of weeks.

The exceptionally late date for Artaxerxes I from Ḥašbâ highlights the importance of only inferring dates of transitions of reign from groups of tablets that all have the same provenance. The result is different dates for different provenances. It is indeed quite possible that Artaxerxes I's reign—whether actual or fictional—ended on different days in different places. The same applies to the beginning of Darius II's reign. Then again, Artaxerxes I's death and Darius II's accession to the throne are historical events. As historical events, they cannot have happened on different days in different places. Consequently, a choice imposes itself. There must be a city where the beginning of the reign of Darius II is closest in time to his actual ascent to the throne as a one-time event. There must be a city whose records are likely to produce the most accurate estimate of the date of Artaxerxes I's death. The obvious choice is Babylon, the premier city of Mesopotamia and at least of equal status as Susa and Persepolis in the Achaemenid empire. But again, some decades ago, the only choice was Nippur. A significant contribution of the two new tablets BM 54557 and Bertin 2889 is that they allow a shift from Nippur to Babylon. Kugler knew of only one relevant tablet from Babylon, no. 2 in §2.4.3.4. The number rose to two by an earlier update (Depuydt 1995a), nos. 2 and 7, and is now again doubled to four, nos. 1, 2, 6, and 7. Evidence from Babylon and Nippur can now be studied separately and priority given to Babylon.

Kugler's interpretation of the return of "Year 41" in dating formulas from Darius II's accession year not only points to 425/24 B.C.E. as the time of Artaxerxes I's death. It also allows, as Kugler fully realized, a more precise calibration of the time of death in early 424 B.C.E. The time derived from the evidence below differs from times derived earlier (Kugler 1907-24, vol. 2.2.2: 397; Depuydt 1995a: 92) for two reasons: (1) new evidence; (2) more precision in the process of derivation.

The point of departure of the process of derivation is the interval in 423 B.C.E. between the latest instance of the dating formula "Accession Year of Darius (II)" and the earliest instance of the dating formula "Year 41 (of Artaxerxes I), Accession Year of Darius (II)." That interval may be derived from the following tablets from Babylon.

TABLETS FROM BABYLON
Dated to "Accession Year of Darius II" (single date)

    Month 9 Day 29   (*ca.* 10 Jan 423)   *new*   BM 54557
    Month 11 Day 4   (*ca.* 13 Feb 423)   *Kug*   *BE* X no. 1

Dated to "Year 41, Accession Year of Darius II" (double date)

    Month 11 Day 26   (*ca.* 7 Mar 423)   *new*   Bertin 2889
    Month 11 Day 29   (*ca.* 10 Mar 423)   *Dep*   BM 33342

Kug = first adduced in Kugler 1907-24, vol. 2.2.2: 395-97; *Dep* = first used in Depuydt 1995a; *new* = used for the first time.

Only one of these tablets was accessible in Kugler's time. Importantly, none are dated to Month 12 (Addaru). The mention of Month 12 as the year's last might have called the entire calendar year to mind and hence the fact that it had consisted of two portions, Year 41 and Darius II's accession year, triggering in turn the description of the whole calendar year as "Year 41, Accession Year of Darius II." I believe certain combinations of "Year 41" with "Accession Year of Darius II" need to be explained in this way.

Kugler's method for deriving the date of Artaxerxes I's death in early 424 B.C.E. from tablets dated to early 423 B.C.E. is unlike anything else in the field of chronology. For clarity's sake, it may be articulated into the following steps. All the dates cited in the three steps fall in early 423 B.C.E.

Step One: On which Babylonian date did "Year 41" reappear in early 423 B.C.E.?—Three dating formulas were used in business documents. In a first period, "Year 41 of Artaxerxes"; in a second period, "Accession Year of Darius"; in a third, "Year 41, Accession Year of Darius." In other words, "Year 41" vanished and then reappeared. The day on which it reappeared cannot be determined exactly. It is one day in a period of which the length is determined as follows.

The period's earliest date is the first day *after* the date of the last instance of "Accession Year of Darius II." The date of that last instance is Month 11 Day 4, that is, *ca.* 13 February, in *BE* X no. 1. Accordingly, the period's earliest date is Month 11 Day 5, that is, *ca.* 14 February. The period's latest date is the date of the earliest attested instance of "Year 41." That date is Month 11 Day 26 in Bertin 2889, that is, *ca.* 7 March.

In sum, "Year 41" reappeared on *a day of the 22-day period lasting from Month 11 Day 5 to Month 11 Day 26, both dates inclusive.*

Relying on the available evidence, Kugler obtained the month-long interval between Month 11 Day 15 and Month 12 Day 14. He does not specify how "between" (*zwischen*) needs to be understood, whether either or both dates are inclusive. The two dates are those of tablets nos. 5 and 8 in the list in §2.4.3.4, *BE* X nos. 3 and 4. Using a newly emerged tablet, I earlier (Depuydt 1995a) obtained an interval about half as long between Month 11 Day 15 and Month Day 29. These two dates are those of tablets nos. 5 and 7 in the same list, *BE* X no. 3 and BM 33342. But in one crucial respect, my shorter interval is less satisfactory than Kugler's longer one because it is evidence from Nippur and Babylon.

Step Two: On which day was Artaxerxes I's reign last recognized, presumably at or shortly after his death, in early 424 B.C.E.?—The Babylonian month and day date is that of the day *preceding* the one on which "Year 41" first reappears in early 423 B.C.E. "Year 41" presumably reappears because using "Accession Year of Darius" just by itself might be misunderstood. On the Babylonian calendar day that precedes the Babylonian calendar day on which "Year 41" reappears in early 424 B.C.E., Artaxerxes I's reign had ended in his Year 40 in early 423 B.C.E. Any Babylonian calendar day in early 423 B.C.E. whose Babylonian calendar date falls later than the Babylonian month and day in early 424 B.C.E. that was the last of Artaxerxes I's reign might, in the absence of "Year 41," follow the Babylonian calendar day of the end of Artaxerxes I's reign a year earlier.

"Year 41" reappears in early 423 B.C.E. on a day in the 22-day period lasting from Month 11 Day 5 to Month 11 Day 26 (see above). The last day on which Artaxerxes I's reign was still recognized in early 424 B.C.E. is therefore *a day in the 22-day period lasting from Month 11 Day 4 to Month 11 Day 25, that is, ca. 26 Jan–ca. 16 Feb 424 B.C.E.*

If "Year 41" first reappears on Month 11 Day 5, then Artaxerxes I's reign ended on Month 11 Day 4 and Month 11 Day 5 was the first calendar day on which misunderstanding was possible. If "Year 41" first reappears on Month 11 Day 26, then Artaxerxes I's reign ended on Month 11 Day 25 and Month 11 Day 26 was the first calendar day on which misunderstanding was possible.

Step Three: What happened in Babylon on the day after the last day of Artaxerxes I's actual reign in Babylon in early 424 B.C.E.?—Documents kept being dated according to Year 41 of Artaxerxes I until at least December 424 B.C.E. A note of his death or of whatever way his reign ended was entered into the historical and astronomical records of the city of Babylon indicating that the actual reign of Artaxerxes I had ended. Such notices are the rule. They have been discussed in detail in §2.4.4. Scribes dating documents in early 423 B.C.E. would have had access to records that laconically stated the date of Artaxerxes I's death. They knew that the accession year of a king begins the day after the day of his predecessor's death. And they knew that a month and day date in Darius II's accession year could be interpreted by later scribes as having followed soon after the actual death of Artaxerxes I rather than a year later.

Can the evidence from Nippur listed in §2.4.3.4 above still contribute to the matter of dating Artaxerxes I's death? If Artaxerxes I died in early 424 B.C.E., the news should surely have arrived everywhere in Mesopotamia by early 423 B.C.E., including at Nippur. Accordingly, as soon as scribes at Nippur learned about Darius II's accession, they could have reintroduced "Year 41" on the same date as at Babylon. If that was indeed the case, the period in early 423 B.C.E. from which the date of Artaxerxes I's death has been derived above could be halved from 22 days to 11 days. Instead of lasting from Month 11 Day 5 to Month 11 Day 26 in early 423 B.C.E., it would last from Month 11 Day 16 to Month 11 Day 26. The beginning would move from Month 11 Day 5 to Month 11 Day 16 because of the date Month 11 Day 15 found in two tablets from Nippur, *BE* X nos. 2 and 3. The same reduction of 11 days would apply to the period in which Artaxerxes I's reign ended, presumably at his death. His death could now be dated to a day in the period lasting from Month 11 Day 15 to Month 11 Day 25 in early 424 B.C.E., that is, *ca.* 6 Feb–*ca.* 16 Feb 424 B.C.E. On the other hand, if Nippur took orders from Babylon regarding the reintroduction of "Year 41" and these orders arrived with delay, the shortening just described would not be permissible.

2.6. The Date of Darius II's Accession: A Day in *ca.* 25 Dec 424 B.C.E.–*ca.* 10 Jan 423 B.C.E.

Briant (2001: 90 note 160) observes that BM 54577 allows "surtout une précision sur la date de la mort d'Artaxerxès (entre mi-décembre 424 et le tout début de 423) et donc sur celle de l'avènement d'Ochos." I would agree with the second half of this statement. My views in relation to the first half are laid out above. BM 54557 definitely permits a refinement of the date of Darius II's accession. According to BM 54557, Darius II was on the throne at the latest by Month 9 Day 29 in early 423 B.C.E., that is, *ca.* 10 January. The latest date for Artaxerxes I's Year 41 is Month 9 Day 12 in late 424 B.C.E., that is, *ca.* 24 December. But this date is preserved in a tablet from Nippur. If news of the accession reached Nippur from Babylon and perhaps also Babylon from Susa with a delay, Darius II would have ascended the throne a little earlier than 25 Dec 424 B.C.E.

2.7. Xerxes II and Sekyndianos

It has been proposed above that the end of Artaxerxes I's reign was acknowledged on a day in the period lasting from Month 11 Day 4 to Month 11 Day 25 in early 424 B.C.E., that is, *ca.* 26 Jan–*ca.* 16 Feb 424 B.C.E. Ktesias, as cited by Photios (see §2.1), reports that Xerxes (II) succeeded Artaxerxes I. If Xerxes II came to the throne the day after his father died, the first full day of his rule would fall in the period lasting from Month 11 Day 5 to Month 11 Day 26 in early 423 B.C.E., that is, *ca.* 27 Jan–*ca.* 17 Feb 424 B.C.E. It seems clear from Ktesias' account that he ruled alone. Ktesias also reports that Xerxes II was murdered after 45 days. If the murder took place on the 45th day of his reign, then the event would have happened at the earliest on Month 12 Day 20 or 21 (depending on whether lunar Month 11 was 30 or 29 days long) and at the latest on Month 13 (second Addaru) Day 11 (if Months 11 and 12 were both 30 days long), 12 (if either month was 29 days long and the other 30), 13 (if Months 11 and 12 were both 29 days long). In short: A day in the period lasting from Month 12 Day 20/21 to Month 13 Day 11/12/13 in early 424 B.C.E., that is, *ca.* 12/13 Mar–*ca.* 2/3/4 Apr 424 B.C.E. Among the eclipse possibilities listed in the Saros Cycle text preserved in BM 36910 + 36998 + 37036 (Aaboe and others 1991: 4–8; cf. *PD* 9) is one for the full moon of Month 13 (second Addaru) of Year 40 of Artaxerxes I (*PD* 9). Xerxes II should already have been murdered by then.

The Greek sources give Xerxes II's successor Sekyndianos six and a half to seven months. He would accordingly have ruled until about September to October 424 B.C.E. From Ktesias' account, one has the impression that his reign may have overlapped with Darius II's. Darius II was probably first recognized in Babylon in the following December or January. The transition from Sekyndianos to Darius II was the most troubled chapter of the whole episode. Instability may have culminated around November of 424 B.C.E.

2.8. Two Excursuses Involving Artaxerxes I and Darius II

2.8.1. Darius II's "Year 13" in Thucydides VIII 58

Thucydides (VIII 58) quotes the text of a treaty between Persia and Sparta. The text of the treaty includes its date, Year 13 of Darius II. The treaty is otherwise known to have taken place in the winter of 412/11 B.C.E., not too long before the end of Thucydides' winter, early March. This treaty of Year 13 therefore also preceded the beginning of Darius II's Babylonian Year 13 on *ca*. 29 Mar 411 B.C.E. Therefore, Year 13 is either a mistake or it is not the Babylonian regnal year. I have elsewhere discussed this chronological problem (Depuydt 1995c: 194–95). Evidence from tablet BM 54557 allows a refinement of my conclusions. Thucydides' Year 13 of Darius II well illustrates that no chronological problem is quite like any other.

One hesitates to assume a mistake on the part of Thucydides, especially as he was alive at the time of the event. If the text is correct, then Year 13 cannot be Babylonian. It is not said by which calendars the treaty is dated. One of the two components of the treaty's date is a reference to the current Spartan ephor, Alexippidas, and therefore presumably involves the calendar of Sparta, whatever its precise structure was. When a treaty between two nations is dated in two different ways and one of the two dates follows the calendar of one nation, then it is reasonable to expect that the other date follows the calendar of the other nation. In the treaty at hand between Sparta and Persia, the reference to ephor Alexippidas is a reference to the Spartan calendar. Accordingly, one would expect Year 13 of Darius II as other component of the treaty's date to be a reference involving the Persian calendar, whatever that calendar was.

Two observations apply. First, Darius II was no doubt already in his 13th regnal year before the beginning of his Babylonian Year 13 if one counts in full solar years starting on the day when he came to the throne. Second, the Babylonian regnal year postdating system in which Year 1 does not begin immediately when the king comes to power but only at the first New Year's Day is unusual among the known calendars of the ancient world. The Persians may well have counted regnal years from the day of the king's ascent to the throne. Other indications support this belief (Depuydt 1995c).

When did the treaty take place? The exact date is unknown. But a reasonable argument can be presented that produces the period inside which the treaty could have occurred. That period is delimited by two dates, a *terminus post quem* "time after which" and a *terminus ante quem* "time before which." The period may be said to have lasted from very late 412 B.C.E. to early March 411 B.C.E. Early March as *terminus ante quem* is the end of winter according to Thucydides.

The *terminus post quem* is the day preceding the day on which Darius II's Year 13 began. That day cannot be precisely defined. But the period within which it falls can be defined approximately. What is special therefore about the present case is that the *terminus post quem* has itself a *terminus post quem* and a *terminus ante quem*. New evidence could possibly fix the *terminus post quem* as early as the day that functions as the *terminus post quem* of the *terminus post quem*, not earlier. Or it could fix the *terminus post quem* as late as its own *term ante quem*, not later. It should be added that the *terminus post quem* of the *terminus post quem* and the *terminus ante quem* of the *terminus post quem* can themselves not be fixed to a precise day, even as they can be conceptualized precisely. In a sense, they too have a *terminus post quem* and *terminus ante quem* in their own right. In a fully developed science of chronology, all these concepts would need to be fully defined.

The *terminus post quem* of the *terminus post quem* is the last day before the day on which the Persian Year 13 of Darius II began. This day can be approximately determined according to the following criteria. The beginning of Year 13 is derived from the beginning of Year 1, or the accession of Darius II. The reign of Artaxerxes I was still recognized in Nippur on Month 9 Day 12, or *ca.* 24 Dec 424 B.C.E. (*PD* 18). Accordingly, Darius II's Year 1 could have begun as early as *ca.* 25 Dec 424 B.C.E., perhaps a little earlier, considering the two possible delays with which the news of the accession could have reached Babylon from the capital in Persia and Nippur from Babylon. Darius II's Year 13 could therefore have begun around the same time in 412 B.C.E. or, again, possibly a little earlier. Month 9 Day 12 is *ca.* 13 December 412 B.C.E. But it is not known how the anniversary of the accession was determined in Persia or how months and days were counted inside a year in the Persian calendar. Accordingly, it is not possible to define the *terminus post quem* of the *terminus post quem* more precisely than very late 424 B.C.E.

The contribution of the tablet BM 54557 to the dating of the treaty between Sparta and Persia is as follows. It allows much greater precision with regard to the range of the *terminus post quem* of the treaty, reducing that range to a month or less. It moves the acknowledgment of the beginning of the reign of Darius II in Babylon to earlier in time by 49–51 days, from lunar Month 11 Day 4 (*PD* 18) to Month 9 Day 29 (the date of BM 54557), or *ca.* 10 Jan 423 B.C.E. The change is 49 days if both Months 9 and 10 had 29 days, 51 days if both Months 9 and 10 had 30 days, and 50 days if one month had 29 days and the other 30 days. Some equivalent of this date in 412/11 B.C.E. is the *terminus ante quem* of the *terminus post quem*.

Accordingly, the *terminus ante quem* of the *terminus post quem* comes closer to the *terminus post quem* of the *terminus post quem* by about 49–51 days. The latter is Month 9 Day 12, in the winter of 412/11 B.C.E. The two would therefore be removed from another by only 17 days. However, that margin in its entirety may belong earlier in time because of the possible delays with which the news could have reached Babylonia from the capital in Persia. Furthermore, the margin could be wider because the earlier date is derived from a tablet from Nippur and the later date from a tablet from Babylon. Typically, one might expect the news to reach the capital city of Babylon earlier than Nippur. It is also not clear how that margin would be transformed by being transferred to 411 B.C.E.

Anticipating the emergence of new evidence, I made (1995c: 195) a statement that begs subtle refinement. I stated that "[an]y date earlier . . . for the anniversary of [Darius II's] accession [derived from cuneiform tablets] would just increase the span of time in which the treaty could have happened." Instead, the new evidence would rather increase "the span of time whose days would with certainty remain possible days of the treaty regardless of future additional evidence from cuneiform tablets." In other words, new evidence would only lengthen the period and could not shorten it.

2.8.2. Day 1 of Judaism: 24 Tishri (*ca.* 30 Oct?) of 445 B.C.E.

Among the Achaemenid emperors, Artaxerxes I seems like a less familiar figure on the stage of world history than his predecessors in spite of his long reign. Cyrus' conquest of Babylon is lauded in the Bible. Ancient history books prominently mention Cambyses' conquest of Egypt. Darius I and Xerxes I endure in modern memory owing to their wars with the Greeks, including the battles at Marathon and Salamis. But "[w]ith the accession of Artaxerxes I," writes Briant (2002 [1996]: 568), "the historian faces a continual dwindling of *narrative* evidence." Yet more than a century ago, Artaxerxes I's role in history has found an eloquent and most erudite advocate in Eduard Meyer. According to Meyer (1896), it was the missions from Susa to Jerusalem on which Artaxerxes I sent Ezra and Nehemiah (pp. 70–71) and the authority with which he backed them that laid the foundation of Judaism (p. 4) and hence of the larger monotheistic tradition encompassing Judaism, Christianity, and Islam. Meyer (1896: 243) concludes his long investigation of Judaism as a "product of the Persian empire" by stating, "[S]o reichen die Wirkungen des Achämenidenreichs gewaltig wie wenig anderes noch unmittelbar in unsere Gegenwart hinein."

Meyer no doubt recognized that many other influences besides Artaxerxes I's contribution, some going back centuries, profoundly shaped Judaism. In that sense, no religious or political institution is born in a short span of time, let alone a single day. Then again, the births of nations are celebrated on well-defined days commemorating a certain event. The interpretation of the formal adoption of the Declaration of Independence on July 4 in 1776 as Day 1 made it possible to celebrate the 200th anniversary of the United States of America in 1976. But obviously, it took much more than this formal adoption to create the U.S.A. By that reasoning, what happened in the preceding centuries might be styled as the Israelite tradition whose legacy served as the bedrock of Judaism.

Does any day present itself as Day 1 of Judaism and therefore of the monotheistic tradition at the beginning of which it stands? A straightforward reading of the Bible leaves little doubt that there is no more suitable day than the "twenty-fourth day of this month" mentioned in Nehemiah 9:1, when "the people of Israel were assembled with fasting and in sackcloth, and with earth on their heads," and declared, "Because of all this we make a firm agreement in writing, and on that sealed document are inscribed the names of our officials, our Levites, and our priests" (Neh 9:38). The translation is the NRSV's.

It was by all accounts a grandiose day, unlike any other in the history of Israel. From what precedes, it is obvious that "this month" of Nehemiah 9:1 is "Month 7" (Tishri) (see Neh 7:73, 8:2). The preceding Month 1 ("Nisan") is dated to "Artaxerxes I's Year 20" (Neh 2:1). Whether his Year 1 is counted from the first Babylonian new year of the reign on 1 Nisanu, that is, *ca.* 13 Apr 464 B.C.E. (see *PD* 32), or from the king's accession to the throne, presumably on a day in August of 465 B.C.E. (see *PD* 17), the "Nisan" or Month 1 of "Year 20" in Nehemiah 2:1 begins—definitely in Babylon and presumably also in Jerusalem—on *ca.* 13 Apr 445 B.C.E. But perhaps, Nisan fell one lunar cycle earlier in Jerusalem, beginning around 15 Mar 465 B.C.E.

I have elsewhere (Depuydt 1995c: 196) proposed that "Year 20 Month 1" in Nehemiah 2:1 follows accession dating because, earlier in the text, at Nehemiah 1:1, Month 7 ("Kislev") also belongs to Year 20. Month 7 should have been part of Year 19 if Babylonian regnal year counting had been used. Kislev (Month 7) in the fall and Nisan (Month 1) in the spring would follow one another in a single regnal year if regnal years are counted from the beginning of the reign in August of 465 B.C.E. I found out later that both Meyer (1896: 92 note 3) and Kugler (1922: 24) had already assumed that regnal years are counted in Ezra and Nehemiah "according to royal years" (*nach Königsjahren*) (Meyer), that is, "from the beginning of the reign" (*vom Regierungsantritt*) (Kugler). According to accession dating, a new regnal year begins at each anniversary of the accession to the throne.

At any event, if the text of the Bible is taken at face value, there is no more suitable day as Day 1 of Judaism than lunar Month 7 Day 24 (24 Tishri) of Year 20 of Artaxerxes I (cf. Meyer 1896: 242). Kugler (1922: 223–26) vigorously defended its historicity. Both he (p. 226) and *PD* 32 compute that daylight of 24 Tishri was 31 Oct 445 B.C.E., a Friday, on the assumption that the first crescent was first visible in the evening of 30 October. For reasons that cannot be detailed here (cf. Depuydt 2002: 171–77), I believe that ancient lunar months could also begin slightly before first crescent visibility, especially in Jerusalem. I would on those grounds personally not exclude daylight of 30 Oct 445 B.C.E., a Thursday, as daylight of 24 Tishri. If Nisan fell a month earlier in Jerusalem, the date would be 30 September. Moving the events of daylight of 24 Tishri to daylight of 1 November does not seem possible because it was a Sabbath.

24 Tishri of 445 B.C.E. may be called the *traditional* date of Day 1 of Judaism. It results from accepting the traditional text of the Bible as it stands. How close to the actual date this traditional date is depends on how reliable the Bible is as a historical source. If the source for 24 Tishri of 445 B.C.E. had been a contemporary document and not a text of literary purport, 24 Tishri of 445 B.C.E. would also have been the actual date. It remains distinctly possible that the traditional date was also the actual date. There has been much discussion on the chronology of Ezra and Nehemiah (cf. Briant 2002 [1996]: 976). According to one view, Nehemiah 9:1–5, and hence also the date of 24 Tishri, may well belong between Ezra 10:15 and 10:16. If so, the events of 24 Tishri would lose some of their splendor and belong in Year 7 of Artaxerxes I, in which 24 Tishri corresponds to *ca.* 25 Oct 458 B.C.E., at least in the Babylonian calender.

3. FROM DARIUS II TO ARTAXERXES II (405/4)

Essence of the Update.—No one has doubted for some time now that Artaxerxes II must have had an accession year. Positive proof has now emerged that he did. The best approximation of the change of rule otherwise remains the period from *ca.* 17 Sep 405 B.C.E. to *ca.* 10 Apr 404 B.C.E. (Depuydt 2006a: 283 note xxiii).

It has long been certain that Year 1 of Artaxerxes II began on *ca.* 10 Apr 404 B.C.E., New Year's Day in Babylon. It was also assumed that he had had an accession year before that, unless Darius II died on the day before new year and Artaxerxes I came to power on new year itself. The existence of Artaxerxes II's accession year is now certain owing to the fragmentary tablet BE 55953 found at the Kasr at Babylon and known only from photographs (Stolper 1999: 6; cf. Boiy 2002a: 27). It is dated to "Year 19, Accession Year of Artaxerxes." There is no month and day date. Only the reign of the second ruler by the name Artaxerxes follows a reign of 19 years, Darius II's.

There remained the remote possibility that Persian kings had stopped using accession years with the reign of Artaxerxes II and henceforth counted their Year 1 when they came to the throne and their Year 2 from the Babylonian new year in the spring. If such had been the case, Darius II could have ruled until after *ca.* 10 Apr 404 B.C.E. Artaxerxes II would then have come to the throne after that Babylonian new year but before the Egyptian new year of 2 Dec 404 B.C.E. The earliest date for Artaxerxes II is in fact Month 1 Day 21 of Year 1, that is, *ca.* 30 Apr 404 B.C.E., the date of the unpublished tablet BE 55770 (Stolper 1999: 6). Ptolemy's Royal Canon would then have predated the beginning of the reign to 2 Dec 405 B.C.E. from that day between the Babylonian new year and Month 1 Day 21, instead of from the Babylonian new year of *ca.* 10 Apr 404 B.C.E. as it in fact does. The remote possibility in question is now definitively eliminated by the evidence derived from BE 55953 (Boiy 2002a: 27).

Ktesias, as cited by Photios (König 1972: 22 §56), writes in Book 19 of his *Persika* that Darius II "died after having becoming sick in Babylon" (ἀπέθανεν ἀσθενήσας ἐν Βαβυλῶνι). It would be difficult to conceive of a better-placed source for a report about a medical condition affecting Darius II. In his *Persika*, Ktesias describes certain events in which "Ktesias himself who was personal physician to Parysatis (Darius II's wife)" (Κτησίας αὐτὸς ἰατρὸς ὢν Παρυσάτιδος) (König 1972: 25 §60) played a role. Photios states that Ktesias "flourished" (ἤκμασε) "in the times of Cyrus son of Darius (II) and Parysatis, who happened to be the brother of Artaxerxes II to whose share the Persian kingdom fell" (ibid.: 1 §1).

I add in appendix about Artaxerxes II that van der Spek (1998) has investigated what can be inferred about his wars from the cuneiform astronomical diaries.

4. FROM ARTAXERXES II TO ARTAXERXES III (359/58)

Essence of the Update.—The period in which the transition occurred is reduced at the end by about one lunar month plus two to three days, or about 32 days, from *ca.* 25 Nov 359 B.C.E.–*ca.* 11 Apr 358 B.C.E. to *ca.* 25 Nov 359 B.C.E.–10 Mar 359 B.C.E. That is a reduction from about 138 days to about 106 days.

Tablet BM 71537 (Walker 1997: 22; Hunger 2001: 40–45 [no. 11]) lists solar eclipse possibilities and apparently belongs to the genre of the Solar Saros Cycle text (for another exemplar, see Aaboe and others 1991: 24–31). Eclipse possibilities occur at five-month or six-month intervals, with a five-month interval being preceded and followed by seven or eight six-month intervals. The transition of reign at hand is mentioned after the solar eclipse possibility of 15 Sep 359 B.C.E. at about 11:51 p.m., as Walker (1997: 22) notes, and before the one of 11 Mar 359 B.C.E., at about 8:52 p.m., as Hunger (2001: 44) observes. The times are Goldstine's (1973: 54). They are the times of conjunction or new moon, when solar eclipses take place. Neither eclipse could be seen at Babylon because the sun had set.

The tablet is very fragmentary. The reference to the earlier eclipse possibility and any possible reference to the end of Artaxerxes II's reign are lost. It has already been noted above that, in Briant's assessment of the collective sources, the transition appears to have been regular (§2.4.4). At least, this can be taken to imply that the surviving sources do not hint at any irregularities. What is left of the text is as follows:

    II′ Obv.
        1′   [....] sat on the throne.

        2′   [Month 11, Day 2]8, ..., omitted.

        3′–4′   (*blank*)

        5′   Year 1 of Umakuš (Ochos) (*and so on*)

The inner logic of the tablet requires that the eclipse of Month 11 Day 28 (of Artaxerxes III's accession year) be preceded by a mention of the eclipse possibility of 15 Sep 359 B.C.E., six conjunctions earlier (Walker 1997:22; but for "15 November" read "15 September," which the author also originally must have meant to write as the conjunction of November falls on the 14th and not the 15th day of the month). The inner logic of the text also indicates that the interval in question must be one of six months and not five months because a five-month interval is mentioned soon after in the text, at II′ Rev. 5–9, from Month 11 of Year 2 to Month 3 of Year 3. Year 2 had a Month 13. The text is continuous from Obverse to Reverse.

The latest known text dated to Artaxerxes II is "still" (Stolper 1999: 5) the Berlin tablet *VAS* VI 186 dated to 25 Nov 359 B.C.E. (*PD* 19). The solar eclipse tablet BM 71537 by inference refers to the second latest date and therefore at least helps consolidating that the transition occurred *after* the first five months of the Babylonian calendar year. BM 71537 is obviously also the earliest known date of Artaxerxes III's reign.

5. FROM ARTAXERXES III TO ARSES (338)

Essence of the Update.—The period in which the transition occurred is reduced from an entire Babylonian calendar year to one lunar month, from the Babylonian calendar year that lasted from spring 338 B.C.E. to spring 337 B.C.E. to lunar Month 6 of that year, that is, *ca.* 27 Aug–*ca.* 25 Sep 338 B.C.E.

According to tablet BM 71537, at III´ Rev. 8–10, Artaxerxes III died and his son Arses (Artaxerxes IV) succeeded him in Month 6 (Ululu) of Artaxerxes I's year 21, that is, *ca.* Aug 27–*ca.* Sep 25 338 B.C.E. (Walker 1997: 21–22; Hunger 2001: 42, 45 [no. 11]). The statement in lines 9–10, $^{1}\acute{U}$-*ma-kuš* NAM^{me} | *Ár-šú* DUMU-*šú ina* AŠ-TE TUŠ-*ab* "Umakuš (Ochos) died. Aršu (Arses), his son, sat on the throne," does not suggest anything special about the transition. The classical sources otherwise leave no doubt that the mighty courtier Bagoas murdered Artaxerxes III, as he later also would his son and successor Arses (see §6) (cf. Briant 2002 [1996]: 688 top, 769).

6. FROM ARSES TO DARIUS III (336/35)

Essence of the Update.—The date of an Aramaic papyrus makes it possible to shorten the full Babylonian calendar year beginning *ca.* 9 Apr 336 B.C.E. in which the transition occurred by about ten days at the end so as to move the *terminus ante quem* back from its last day, *ca.* 28 Mar 335 B.C.E., to *ca.* 18 Mar 335 B.C.E. An observation in Diodoros probably allows moving the *terminus post quem* by a few months from the Babylonian new year of *ca.* 9 Apr 336 B.C.E. to about late summer, August 336 B.C.E. or so.

An Aramaic papyrus from Wadi Daliyeh (see Gropp 2001: 33–44; cf. Boiy 2002a: 28 note 20 and Briant 2002 [1996]: 714) is dated to Month 12 (Adar) Day 20 of "Year 2 (of Arses), accession year of Darius (III)," that is, *ca.* 19 Mar 335 B.C.E. Arses (Artaxerxes IV) could therefore have reigned until as late as the previous day, Month 12 Day 19, that is, *ca.* 18 Mar 335 B.C.E. The increase in precision in dating his reign is small. The period in which the succession occurred has been shortened by 10 days in that its end is moved back in time from the day before new year, that is, *ca.* 28 Mar 335 B.C.E., to *ca.* 18 Mar 335 B.C.E.

Further shortening by a few months may be possible on the basis of the following considerations. Diodoros (XVII 5,4) writes that Arses had a third year, it being in that year that the powerful courtier Bagoas killed him. Arses ascended the throne around September 338 B.C.E. (§5). It is not known with certainty how Diodoros counted his years. Two likely possibilities are, (1), by full solar years from the accession, and (2), from summer to summer as in Olympiad and Athenian archon reckoning. Diodoros hardly employed Egyptian predating. Accordingly, it is difficult to imagine by what method of year-counting the beginning of Arses' Year 3 could have begun earlier than about September 336 B.C.E., exactly two years after his accession in about September 338 B.C.E. Africanus and Eusebius support Diodoros' report that Arses' reign was longer than two years by giving the length of his reign as three and four years respectively (cf. Lloyd 1988 and 1994: 359–60). Four years seems long, however, if one considers the cuneiform record and the fact that his reign is two Egyptian years long in Ptolemy's Royal Canon. Accordingly, the transition of reign would have occurred between about September 336 B.C.E. at the earliest to 18 Mar 335 B.C.E.

From Ptolemy's Royal Canon, it can be inferred that the Babylonian year lasting from spring 336 B.C.E. to spring 335 B.C.E. encompassed both Arses' Year 2, his last, and the accession year of Darius III. Accordingly, it has been generally assumed that Darius III had had an accession year. The afore-mentioned Aramaic papyrus and cuneiform tablet HSM 1893.5.29 now both confirm this in the flesh (Boiy 2002a: 28). Only one later king had an accession year, Alexander III (see below). The accession year was abandoned starting with Philip Arridaios. The absence of an accession year in cuneiform tablets only applies to king Arridaios, general Antigonos the One-Eyed, and king Alexander IV, and king Seleukos I. After them, there were no longer beginnings of reigns because the Seleucid Era came into use.

7. FROM DARIUS III TO ALEXANDER III (332–30)

Essence of the Update.—Only in recent years has it become possible to gain a comprehensive picture of all the various ways in which years came to be counted simultaneously in daily life when Alexander conquered the Achaemenid empire. In Ptolemy's Royal Canon, the year count is partly artificial and designed for use by astronomers. The Canon switches from rulers of Babylon to rulers of Alexandria with Alexander III, Philip Arridaios, and Alexander IV, who ruled both Babylon and Alexandria. The Canon's switch from Babylonia to Egypt can now be placed fairly securely at the beginning of Alexander III's reign.

No personality of antiquity is more famous than Alexander the Great. Still, it has taken until recently for a nearly complete picture to emerge of the ways in which his regnal years were counted in Macedonia, Egypt, and Babylonia—to name the nations that were home to the three dominant calendars of his time—and also of how these ways of counting relate to one another historically and chronologically. The reigns of Alexander and his two successors, his half-brother Philip Arridaios and his son Alexander IV, are unlike anything else in chronology. These three reigns were fully officially and yet fully separately dated according to all three calendars just mentioned. Moreover, the reigns are also included in Ptolemy's Royal Canon, adding a fourth way to date Alexander's reign (Depuydt 1995d). Many chronological issues affect the early Hellenistic years 332 B.C.E.–304 B.C.E. They cannot be addressed in detail here (see now Boiy 1998, 2000, 2001, 2002a, and 2002b [with references to all prior pertinent investigations]; see also Wheatley 1998 and 2002). The present section concerns a brief survey of regnal year counting in Alexander's reign, which now appears to have emerged in full profile from the mists of time.

There are five ways of counting Alexander's years. In the order in which they came into existence, they are as follows:

        (1) Macedonian;
        (2) Egyptian;
        (3) Babylonian in documentary and astronomical texts;
        (4) Babylonian in astronomical Saros texts;
        (5) derived from Egyptian in Ptolemy's Canon.

The manner in which these five ways relate to one another will be presented here for the sake of clarity in narrative mode, making the institution of the year counts themselves into historical events. The five ways of counting years involve three types of calendar years, each with its own beginning. The Macedonian year began in the fall. In the period at hand, the Egyptian year began about two months later on 14 November in 332–30 B.C.E., on 13 November in 329–26 B.C.E., and on 12 November in 325–23 B.C.E. The Babylonian new year followed about four to five months later in the spring.

In the transition from Darius III to Alexander III, the following happened in terms of years counts. In or around the fall of 332 B.C.E., Alexander had ruled Macedonia for about four full solar years. In 332 B.C.E., the Macedonian calendar year began around the new moon of 17 September according to Grzybek (1990: 58). Alexander's father Philip II of Macedonia had been murdered about four years earlier. No documents have survived in which Alexander's reign is dated according to Macedonian years. It therefore remains uncertain how he counted these years officially. That uncertainty also affects the time of year when the regnal years began and ended. In Alexander's case, his accession to the throne presumably fell close to the beginning of the Macedonian calendar year in the fall. It is tempting to think that regnal years began exactly with new year. But that need not have been the case. Each year Alexander might have remembered the date of his ascension to the throne, even if it was close to new year, and changed the number of his regnal year on that date. In light of the uncertainty, I will count Alexander's Macedonian reign by full years that have elapsed since the approximate date of his accession around September/October 336 B.C.E.

In the fall of 332 B.C.E., Alexander was close to or right before Gaza, his siege of which lasted about two months (Diodoros XVII 48,7). At this point, his years were still counted by just one system. After taking Gaza, Alexander reached Pelusium in Egypt in seven days (Arrian, *Anabasis*, III 1,1). The Egyptian new year fell on 14 November in 332 B.C.E. It cannot be inferred from the sources with certainty whether

Alexander conquered Egypt before 14 November or after. Most calibrations would probably lead to the conclusion that it had been rather close. Beloch (1923: 314–15)—whose handling of chronology is, among all those who wrote Greek histories, the most delicate, just as Eduard Meyer's was among those who wrote histories of the ancient world in general—believes it happened in late November. But that is an inference from Ptolemy's Canon. The Canon predates and its Year 1 begins on 14 Nov 332 B.C.E. If the Canon predates here as it otherwise normally does elsewhere, then the actual beginning of the reign ought to fall after 14 November. The surviving narrative sources do not allow a conclusion about the precise date of arrival in Egypt. I have the impression that an arrival after 14 November is altogether likely, considering what all happened. But positive proof is lacking. Very little is known about the chronology of the few months that Alexander spent in Egypt.

At all events, there is no doubt that Alexander's Egyptian Year 2 is counted from new year of 14 Nov 331 B.C.E. But when did scribes begin dating documents by his Year 1? Gauthier (1916: 199 note 1) already noted that it is "pas facile à dire" but, among the options he proposes, Darius III's death in 330 B.C.E. (Briant 2002 [1996]: 864–66) is definitely too late. A principal difficulty is that there are no Egyptian documents dated to the end of Darius III's reign and the beginning of Alexander's reign. As far as I know, the latest year date for Darius III is Year 2 (335/34 B.C.E.) Month 4 in Demotic papyrus Louvre E 2430 (Kienitz 1953: 231) and the earliest dates for Alexander are Year 3 Month 1 Day 1 in a graffito in the temple at Luxor (Gauthier 1916: 199) and Month 3 (330/29 B.C.E.) in Demotic papyrus Louvre E 2439 (Gauthier 1916: 200; Pestman 1967: 11). To my knowledge, only four dates belonging to Alexander's reign have come to light. Only one, the graffito at Luxor, specifies day, month, and year; the three others, just the month in addition to the year. A date in Year 9 is mentioned below. A Buchis stela dated to Month 1 of Alexander's Year 4 has also survived (Mond and Myers 1934, vol. 1: 3 [read "Thoth" (Month 1) for "Paopi" (Month 2)], vol. 3: Plate XXVII). [See now Boiy 2007: 35–36 (eight dates, five more, not the graffito).] "

But at issue is what happened from November 332 B.C.E. to November 331 B.C.E. in terms of year-dating. There are two basic possibilities. First, Alexander became Pharaoh a little before the Egyptian new year of 14 November 332 B.C.E. but waited until new year to begin his Year 1. Second, Alexander began his Egyptian Year 1 officially at some point after 14 November and it lasted until 13 Nov 331 B.C.E. In this case, Darius III's Egyptian Year 5 could still have begun on that same New Year's Day. But it is not known whether any documents were ever dated to his Year 5. It is not clear what might have prompted scribes to begin dating documents by Alexander's Year 1 if they did. Pseudo-Kallisthenes transmits a report that Alexander was crowned according to Egyptian rites at Memphis. According to Skeat (1969: 27), "historians generally reject this story." Even so, it cannot be known whether scribes would have begun dating by Year 1 on the day of the crowning.

Alexander spent several months in Egypt and must have been in Egypt at the Babylonian new year, when Darius III's Babylonian Year 5 began. He left Egypt some time around mid-331 B.C.E., it is not known exactly when. Since he died on 11 Jun 323 B.C.E., Alexander must have had an Egyptian Year 9 beginning on 12 Nov 424 B.C.E. In fact, the Demotic papyrus Strassburg 1 (edited by Spiegelberg 1902 and Glanville 1939: xxvii–xxxvi) is dated to Month 1 of his Year 9, that is 12 Nov–11 Dec 324 B.C.E. Gauthier (1916: 195 note) mentions the papyrus in a footnote to his section on Pharaoh Khababash (*Ḫbbš*) because the same scribe who wrote Papyrus Strassburg 1 dated to Year 9 of Alexander also wrote Papyrus Libbey (Spiegelberg 1907) dated to Month 3 of Year 1 of Pharaoh Khababash.

Alexander could have begun counting his Egyptian years as late as his decisive defeat of Darius III at Gaugamela on 1 Oct 331 B.C.E. and his entry into Babylon soon after. The possibility cannot be excluded, therefore, that he began counting his regnal years at the same time both at Memphis and Babylon. But it seems more likely that he began the official count of his regnal years earlier in Egypt than in Western Asia, even if positive proof is lacking.

At the time of the battle of Gaugamela of 1 Oct 331 B.C.E., Alexander had been ruler of Macedonia for close to five full five Macedonian years. In 331 B.C.E., the Macedonian new year fell on 7 September according to Grzybek (1990: 58). Soon after the battle, Alexander's Babylonian accession year, attested in cuneiform tablet BM 87241 (Boiy 2002a: 30–32; cf. 2000: 118 note 14), began and lasted until the Babylonian new year in the spring of 330 B.C.E. Meanwhile, 12 Nov 331 B.C.E. was Day 1 of his Egyptian Year 2. Alexander the Great was the last king to have a Babylonian accession year (Boiy 2002a).

When the Babylonian new year arrived in the spring of 330 B.C.E., Alexander had clearly ruled Macedonia for about five and a half years. Yet, there is no doubt that he began his Babylonian Year 7 on that day. Presumably, he had two choices. If he began his Year 6 that day, it could seem as if he had reigned only five full years whereas he had definitely reigned five and a half. If he began his Year 7 that day, it could seem as if he had ruled half a year more than he actually did. There was no perfect solution in this sense. Apparently, Alexander chose the latter option. It seems to make sense that he wanted to see the fact that he had reigned more than five years recognized. New year of Alexander's Year 7 was therefore preceded by new year of Darius III's Year 5. A document in which this is explicitly the case is BM 35531 + 45740 (Hunger 2001: 260–77 [no. 66], at 270–71). Importantly, whereas Alexander's Egyptian year count disregards his Macedonian reign, his Babylonian year count includes it.

All this also explains, as Boiy (2002b: 250) observes, why "no contemporary cuneiform documents dating to Alexander's first regnal years were found." "First" can be specified as "1 through 6." In cuneiform documents and colophons in literary tablets, Years 8 to 13 are attested (Boiy 2000: 118). No similar evidence has come to light for his Babylonian Year 7 and his Babylonian Year 14, which Alexander must have both had in Babylon. Alexander's Babylonian reign ranged from Year 7 to Year 14 and was preceded by an accession year. He died at the end of the second month of his Babylonian year 4. By contrast, three Egyptian documents dating to his years 3 and 4 have been cited above.

The progression of Alexander's regnal years may be represented as follows.

ALEXANDER'S REGNAL YEARS AS PHARAOH AND ACHAEMENID EMPEROR

YEAR IN MACEDONIA	FULL YEARS REIGNED (CARDINAL NUMBER)	BABYLONIAN YEAR (ORDINAL NUMBER)	EGYPTIAN (ORDINAL NUMBER)
ca. Sep 336 (succeeds father)	0.00		
late 332 (invades Egypt)	ca. 4.15		1st begins
Oct 331 (after Gaugamela)	ca. 5.00	accession year begins	1st continues
14 Nov 331 (Eg. new year)	ca. 5.15	accession year continues	2nd begins
spring 330 (Bab. new year)	ca. 5.50	7th begins	2nd continues
ca. Sep 330	ca. 6.00	7th continues	2nd continues
14 Nov 330 (Eg. new year)	ca. 6.15	7th continues	3rd begins
spring 329 (Bab. new year)	ca. 6.50	8th begins	3rd continues
ca. Sep 329	ca. 7.00	8th continues	3rd continues
13 Nov 329 (Eg. new year)	ca. 7.15	8th continues	4th begins
spring 328 (Bab. new year)	ca. 7.50	9th begins	4th continues
ca. Sep 328	ca. 8.00	9th continues	4th continues
13 Nov 328 (Eg. new year)	ca. 8.15	9th continues	5th begins
spring 327 (Bab. new year)	ca. 8.50	10th begins	5th continues
ca. Sep 327	ca. 9.00	10th continues	5th continues
13 Nov 327 (Eg. new year)	ca. 9.15	10th continues	6th begins
spring 326 (Bab. new year)	ca. 9.50	11th begins	6th continues
ca. Sep 326	ca. 10.00	11th continues	6th continues
13 Nov 326 (Eg. new year)	ca. 10.15	11th continues	7th begins
spring 325 (Bab. new year)	ca. 10.50	12th begins	7th continues
ca. Sep 326	ca. 11.00	12th continues	7th continues
12 Nov 325 (Eg. new year)	ca. 11.15	12th continues	8th begins
spring 324 (Bab. new year)	ca. 11.50	13th begins	8th continues
ca. Sep 324	ca. 12.00	13th continues	8th continues
12 Nov 324 (Eg. new year)	ca. 12.15	13th continues	9th begins
spring 323 (Bab. new year)	ca. 12.50	14th begins	9th continues

Alexander dies on 11 Jun 323 B.C.E. in his Egyptian Year 9 and his Babylonian Year 14, having reigned about 12 years and 7 to 8 months in all.

The dates in the spring are those of the Babylonian new year. The distance between the Macedonian new year and the Babylonian new year is given at half a year (0.50 years), which is an approximate average. The former began around the fall equinox and the latter around the spring equinox.

The needs of astronomers are different from those of historians. For the practice of astronomy, astronomers like to divest themselves from historical complications such as the specific day on which a king ascended to the throne. Astronomers desire year counts that begin with a full Year 1 and in which each year covers a full calendar year. Such astronomical calendars were created in both Egypt and Babylon, adding two more ways of counting. Such calendars are necessary for theoretical astronomy including the study of cycles over long periods of time. However, when recording celestial events day by day, even astronomers naturally preferred to use the historical calendar. Two year counts for Alexander are therefore attested in Babylonian astronomical texts, the historical one beginning with his Year 7 and the purely astronomical one in which new year of Year 1 is the same as new year of the historical Year 7.

Two counts of Alexander's years were therefore added to the three historical counts already mentioned above, bringing the total to five. The Egyptian historical count already begins with Year 1. It is not clear on what day Year 1 began (see above). In any event, the historical count was converted into a count suitable for astronomical purposes by making new year of 14 Nov 332 B.C.E. into the beginning of Year 1. This is the year count of Ptolemy's Royal Canon (Depuydt 1995d).

In Babylon, Alexander's accession year was counted as part of Darius III's reign, making it seem as if Darius III had ruled Babylon for about half a year after Alexander had occupied the city. As a result, the beginning of Alexander's Year 1 astronomically fell a year and about four to five months later in Babylon than the beginning of the Egyptian Year 1 astronomically did. This count was used in the Solar Saros (Aaboe and others 1991: 24–31) and the (Lunar) Saros Canon (ibid.: 12–22).

COUNTS OF ALEXANDER'S REGNAL YEARS
IN ASTRONOMICAL TEXTS

		BABYLONIAN *Theoretical Babylonian* *Astronomical Texts*	EGYPTIAN *Ptolemy's* *Royal Canon*
14 Nov 322	(Egyptian new year)		1st begins
14 Nov 331	(Egyptian new year)		2nd begins
spring 330	(Babylonian new year)	1st begins	
14 Nov 330	(Egyptian new year)		3rd begins
spring 329	(Babylonian new year)	2nd begins	
13 Nov 329	(Egyptian new year)		4th begins
spring 328	(Babylonian new year)	3rd begins	
13 Nov 328	(Egyptian new year)		5th begins
spring 327	(Babylonian new year)	4th begins	
13 Nov 327	(Egyptian new year)		6th begins
spring 326	(Babylonian new year)	5th begins	
13 Nov 326	(Egyptian new year)		7th begins
spring 324	(Babylonian new year)	6th begins	
12 Nov 325	(Egyptian new year)		8th begins
spring 324	(Babylonian new year)	7th begins	

PHILIP ARRIDAIOS' REIGN

12 Nov 424	(Egyptian new year)		1st begins
spring 323	(Babylonian new year)	1st begins	
12 Nov 324	(Egyptian new year)		2nd begins
spring 322	(Babylonian new year)	2nd begins	
		(*and so on*)	

8. FROM ALEXANDER III TO ARRIDAIOS (323)

Essence of the Update.—This section contains various additional observations on the year, month, day, and hour of Alexander the Great's death, especially in reference to the long and complex history of the study of the date. An even fuller account of the modern history of the chronology of the reign of Alexander remains desirable. What is especially lacking in the present account is a comprehensive treatment of the modern history of the study of ancient Macedonian time-reckoning in Macedonia, Egypt and elsewhere. [See also Appendix II.]

No precision is added to the date Alexander's death itself other than a slight recalibration, according to a more rigorous rationale, of the 60-minute period starting at the top of the hour that is most likely to be closest to all possible hours to the time of death.

8.1. History of the Study of the Date of Alexander's Death

Two centuries after Cambyses' conquest of Egypt, in the late afternoon of 11 June of the year 323 B.C.E., Alexander the Great died in Babylon as ruler of the Achaemenid empire. There was once a time when it was not clear whether Alexander had died in 324 B.C.E. or 323 B.C.E. But the matter has long been settled in favor of 323 B.C.E.

This update of an earlier discussion (Depuydt 1997) is a partly meant as a first step towards gaining more of a bird's eye view of the past study of the date of Alexander's death back from the present all the way to when the event took place. The correct *year* has been in plain view continually from soon after the event itself in antiquity (§8.2). Ideler did much to bring the correct *lunar month* into proper focus (§§8.3–4). The correct *day* and *hour* were fully established only by the mid-1990s (§8.5). Of the earlier paper only what is needed to make the present line of argument whole is repeated here.

The following appreciation of Ideler's crucial role in past research on the time of Alexander's death serves as a correction of my earlier statement (Depuydt 1997: 117) that, "[i]n no modern scholarly work, in fact not even in earlier discussions from the Renaissance onwards, has Alexander's death ever been dated to any other month than June of 323 B.C." It came to my attention soon after this statement was published that the great Petavius in the early seventeenth century had dated the event to 324 B.C.E. Scaliger, both his greatest muse and his greatest abomination, was in this case closer to the truth by dating it to mid-323 B.C.E.

Collecting everything that has ever been said about the dating of Alexander's death in the scholarly literature of the past two centuries would require much work. The task would not be a wasted effort but difficult to accomplish. In my experience, the history of a chronological problem often sheds light on the problem itself. May it suffice to mention the only monograph ever that to my knowledge was exclusively devoted to the key dates of Alexander's life, Rudolf Schrader's doctoral dissertation of 1889 for the University of Bonn, *De Alexandri Magni Vitae Tempore* "On the Time of Alexander the Great's Life," which includes an update of the question of the date of Alexander's death (Schrader 1889: 5–8, 16–23). While acknowledging that Ideler has treated the question "quite fruitfully" (*uberius*) and has thoroughly demonstrated (*optime demonstravit*) that the year was 323 B.C.E. (p. 5), Schrader rejects Ideler's method for obtaining month and day because the Macedonian calendar' structure was not yet sufficiently understood (p. 6) (see below). Instead, he considers 13 Jun 323 B.C.E. to be the date of the event "without any interference from doubt" (*nulla interposita dubitatione*). He infers from Pseudo-Kallisthenes that the Egyptian date had been Month 8 (Pharmouti) Day 4, which in 323 B.C.E. no doubt fell on 13 June. Kallisthenes was Aristotle's nephew who accompanied Alexander in the capacity of reporter and historian. The writings designated as Pseudo-Kallisthenes are only in name his.

The date of 13 June has always been influential, probably owing to the transparency of the Egyptian calendar and the circumstance noted also by Schrader that Alexander was buried in Alexandria in Egypt. According to *PD* 19 note 4, Alexander died on Month 3 (Simanu) Day 1, which is identified with 13 Jun

323 B.C.E. And yet in 1955, *LBART* (Pinches and others 1955) had just appeared, in which the tablet BM 45962 that leaves no doubt that Alexander had died on 11 Jun 323 B.C.E. is published in facsimile (see now Sachs and Hunger 1988: 207) and in the introduction of which the reference to Alexander's death is noted (Pinches and others 1955: xiii). This work is cited repeatedly in *PD*. It is not said how 1 Simanu is obtained. I would provisionally suggest that pressure from the attractive date 13 June may have played a role. One might speculate that, although *PD* deals with Babylonian chronology, the Egyptian date of 13 June may have had special appeal to one of its two authors, Richard A. Parker, as an Egyptologist. Parker was solely responsible for the second edition of *PD* of 1956 (the first appeared in 1942).

Schrader also accepts from Pseudo-Kallisthenes that daylight of that day had been daylight of Day 1 of a lunar month, on the evening before which the first crescent had first been seen. The first crescent could no doubt have been seen by the evening of 12 Jun 323 B.C.E. Conjunction—the time when sun, moon, and earth, in that order, are found on a single line, or better, in a single plane—occurred close to 00:06 a.m. on 11 Jun 323 B.C.E. (Goldstine 1973: 57). Then again, classical sources closer to the event suggest that the death had occurred at the end of a lunar month and not at the beginning.

8.2. The Year: *Year 1 of Olympiad 114 or Olympiad CXIV.4 (324/23 B.C.E.)*

On 24 May 1821, Ludwig Ideler read a paper to the Berlin Academy on the time of death of Alexander. This paper came to my attention shortly after I completed my own study of the matter (Depuydt 1997). No account of the date in question can be complete without considering this pivotal paper by the greatest chronologer of the nineteenth century. The paper's published version commences as follows (1822: 261):

> Die Aufgabe: das julianische Datum des Tages zu bestimmen, an welchem Alexander von Macedonien gestorben ist, gehört zu den schwierigsten, die den Alterthumsforscher beschäftigen können.

It seems worth recalling that it was Ideler who, in his *Historische Untersuchungen* of 1806, established the true foundations for the dating of much of the history of the West in the "BC" period. An adequate grasp of ancient chronology must begin with an understanding of how dates function in Ptolemy's work on astronomy (second century A.D.). Ideler studied all the relevant chronological data and definitively established their coherence and veracity. Only one other work rivals Ideler's *Untersuchungen* in its status as enabler of the first order, namely Paul Crusius' *Liber de epochis* of 1578. Of equally deceptive slimness as Ideler's tome and equally little known, Crusius' *De epochis* brought order to the understanding of the Era of Nabonassar, which is a fundamental component of Ptolemy's dating method. Ancient history is a structure in which elements come in a certain order and certain elements precede others. The chronological sequence of events comes at the very beginning. And nothing, except for Babylonian astronomical records (see Depuydt 2008), comes earlier than what is said in the two afore-mentioned books. It may not be widely realized that AD 1578 and AD 1806 are the dates of the publication of two unrivaled catalysts in the study of antiquity as a highly organized intellectual enterprise (cf. Depuydt 2007: §§2 and 3).

In general, up to Ideler's time, that is, the early nineteenth century, a major divide existed in the writings of leading scholars of chronology. Some assumed that Alexander had died at the beginning of Olympiad CXIV.1, that is, sometime in or near the fall of 324 B.C.E. In addition to Petavius, they include Fréret, Sainte-Croix, and "most French scholars" (Ideler 1822: 263). Others believed that Alexander died at the end of that year, in the early summer of 323 B.C.E. In addition to Scaliger, these include Ussher, Dodwell, Des-Vignoles, and "all German chronologists" (p. 266). Ideler carefully analyzes all the arguments that had been adduced in favor of both points of view. While acknowledging that his investigation has not produced a "completely decisive result" (p. 262) and while exposing flaws in the arguments adduced for both views, Ideler clearly sides with those who date Alexander's death to the end of the year in question and considers the arguments presented in favor of the rival view to be "very weak" (*sehr schwach*) (p. 277).

Unlike so much of "BC" chronology, the year did not rest on the foundation of Ptolemy's Royal Canon (for this document, see Depuydt 1995d). For allowing Alexander's death to be dated to the exact year for the first time since antiquity, gratitude is owed to the ancient chronologers who brought order to the Greek Olympiads in their relation to the list of archons of Athens as a tool of time-reckoning. Tradition gives much credit to the eminent Timaios of Tauromenium (*ca.* 356 B.C.E.–*ca.* 260 B.C.E.), called *longe eruditissimus* "by far the most erudite" by Cicero in his *De oratore* at II 58, perhaps at least partly in reference to his accomplishments in chronology and history. In regard to chronology, one would not want to leave the sterling reputations of Eratosthenes of Cyrene (*ca.* 275 B.C.E.– *ca.* 194 B.C.E.) and his popularizer Apollodoros of Athens (born *ca.* 180 B.C.E.) without mention.

Over the centuries, just about every student of Alexander's death since the time when the event took place more than 2,300 years ago has placed it in the right year-long span, namely the first of the four years of the 114th Olympiad, that is, Olympiad CXIV.1, which lasts from the Olympic games of 324 B.C.E. to the same time in the high to late summer of 323 B.C.E. All this does not mean that the year might not have turned out to be wrong. Not everything that everyone has always believed about the historical past has withstood the test of time. But the year of Alexander's death did. And it could count from the beginning, as Ideler (1822: 262–63) observes, on the unanimous support of all the most reliable sources, including Arrian citing Aristoboulos, Diodoros, and the Armenian version of Eusebios.

Ideler's study had been at least in part prompted by a surprising development. In his *Annales des Lagides ou chronologie des rois grecs d'Égypte* (2 vols., Paris, 1819), Champollion-Figeac devoted 114 pages (vol. 1, pp. 60–173) to a defense of the view that Alexander died at the end of Year 4 of Olympiad 113, or Olympiad CXIII.4, the year before the one in which most everyone else had always believed that he had died. That would place the death in the late spring or early summer of 324 B.C.E. In a postscript, Ideler notes that Champollion-Figeac's theory was severely criticized by Saint-Martin in his *Nouvelles recherches sur l'époque de la mort d'Alexandre et sur la chronologie des Ptolémées* (Paris, 1820). Then again, Saint-Martin too placed Alexander's death in Olympiad CXIII.4.

Without entering into much detail here, Ideler rightly concludes that Champollion-Figeac's investigation is "entirely flawed" (*gänzlich verfehlt*) (p. 284). One illustration of Champollion-Figeac's treatment of the problem may suffice. Although he places Alexander's death in Year 4 of Olympiad 113 and Olympiad CXIII.4 no doubt lasted from summer 325 B.C.E. to summer 324 B.C.E., he nevertheless dates the event to 323 before Christ. Ideler charitably assumes that the year is counted as in astronomy, namely by including a Year 0 between 1 B.C. (or 1 B.C.E.) and A.D. 1 (or 1 C.E.). Champollion-Figeac's "323 before Christ" would then in effect be the same year as astronomy's –323 ("minus 323"), that is, 324 B.C.E. (B.C.). However, Champollion-Figeac throughout his long treatise mixes the two ways of counting years to such a degree without ever explicitly marking the difference that Ideler is right to diagnose an "incomprehensible confusion" (*unbegreifliche Verwirrung*) (p. 282) in all the year-dates of Champollion-Figeac's *Annales des Lagides*.

8.3. The Month and Part of Month:
The Lunar Month Beginning around the Conjunction of 12 May 323 B.C.E., More Precisely Its End

In his abridgment of Pompeius Trogus' *Historiae Philippicae*, widely read in the Middle Ages, at XII 16,1, Justinus (third century C.E.) gives the name of the Julian month correctly as June. But his report is limited in value because it is not clear how he obtained the month. It is owed to the paper Ideler read to the Berlin academy in 1821 and published in 1822 that the correct lunar month in which Alexander had died gained the upper hand in chronological discourse, just after the study of the time of Alexander's death had undergone its severest crisis ever with the appearance of Champollion-Figeac's *Annales des Lagides* and less so with Saint-Martin's *Nouvelles recherches*. Then again, Ideler relied on the structure of the Macedonian lunar calendar and its relation with other ancient lunar calendars. Few problems of ancient chronology exhibit greater complexity. As a result, the exact lunar month in which Alexander died was not as prominent in discussions since Ideler as it could have been if its identification had relied on a less complex argumentation.

Since Ideler, the correct time of Alexander's death has been in focus within a range of five days or so. In the subsequent literature, one finds dates ranging from 9 June to 13 June. Ideler might have been wrong. But his arguments were strong and they have withstood the test of time, especially by being confirmed later by the cuneiform evidence, which only came to light and was deciphered after Ideler's time.

Ideler's defense of the later date involves the structure of the Macedonian lunar calendar. His arguments cannot be addressed in detail here. Our understanding of the Macedonian calendar has much advanced since his time and his understanding of that calendar appears to have been less than perfect. Still, Ideler (1822: 266) was right in accepting Plutarch's equation (*Life of Alexander*, 16) of the Macedonian month of Daisios in which Alexander died with the Athenian month of Thargelion, the Athenian calendar's eleventh, while otherwise assuming that the first Athenian lunar month began around the first conjunction after the summer solstice. That makes the month Thargelion in question the one that begins around 12 May 323 B.C.E. The months of lunar calendars everywhere all mostly overlap because they all follow the same moon. They deviate from another only by one or two days with regard to when they begin or end.

8.4. The (Half-)Day: *Daylight 11 Jun 323 B.C.E.*

I have elsewhere laid out the case for daylight of 11 Jun 323 B.C.E. as the exact half-day—in addition to the hour (see §8.5)—on the basis of a comprehensive review of all the sources, both Near Eastern and classical (Depuydt 1997). I would personally consider 11 June to be as secure as ancient dates of the era "BC"come.

As it happens, Ideler already proposed 11 June in his afore-mentioned paper of 1821, but only as one of two options, 11 June and 13 June. The two options stem from the fact that Aristoboulos and the Royal Diaries, both quoted in Plutarch's *Life of Alexander* (75,6 and 76,9), date the event to two different days of the Macedonian month of Daisios, namely Day 28 and the day called Triakas (τριακάς), which can be either Day 29 or Day 30 depending on whether the lunar month is 29 days or 30 days long. In addition to being merely one of two options, 11 June is obtained by Ideler through a different method involving two assumptions: (1) Meton's cycle was used at the time in Athens to date daily events; (2) the reconstruction of the cycle used by Ideler is correct. Assumption (1) is highly improbable: astronomical cycles were probably not used outside astronomy. If assumption (1) does not apply, then assumption (2) does not either.

8.5. The Hour: *Perhaps rather* ca. *3:00–4:00 p.m. than* ca. *4:00–5:00 p.m.*

I earlier proposed "ca. 4:00–5:00 p.m." by the following rationale (Depuydt 1997: 126). The Royal Diaries quoted in Plutarch's *Life of Alexander* (76,9) describe the time of day as πρὸς δείλην "around δείλη." The ancient sources leave no doubt that *deilē* denotes a period in late afternoon during which the sun is descending in the sky but which is separated from sunset by an interval of time. I considered that period fully captured by the description "3:00–6:00 p.m." and then chose the middle hour while adding "*ca.*" to obtain the single hour that is closest to all the possible hours. But the exact numbers 3:00 p.m. and 6:00 p.m. were not motivated by a rationale that can be described as being as precise as possible.

I might now slightly modify this calculation. The Anecdota Graeca, at I 23 (Bekker), transmit a definition according to which *deilē* denoted the ninth and the tenth hour in Attica. It is not clear how often the ancient Greeks associated *deilē* with specific hours of the day. To the extent that they did, the hours must have been seasonal, changing in length over the course of the year along with the length of the year. Alexander died close to the summer solstice. At Babylon, the day would have been about 14 hours long, lasting from about 5:00 a.m. to about 7:00 p.m. One seasonal hour would have been about 70 minutes long. If one divides daylight time into 12 seasonal hours of 70 minutes, the ninth and tenth hour last from about 2:20 p.m. to about 4:50 p.m. If rounded off to full hours starting at the top of the hours, the period that results is 2:00–5:00 p.m. This time interval is slightly earlier than my approximation of *deilē* as 3:00–6:00 p.m. One might propose 2:00–6:00 to include all possible hours for *deilē* and still leave an interval between the end of *deilē* and sunset at about 7:00 p.m.

The 60-minute period that is statistically closest to all possible times inside the afore-mentioned interval 2:20–4:50 p.m. is the period right in the middle, 3:05–4:05 p.m. The closest 60-minute period starting at the top of the hour is 3:00–4:00 p.m. We do not know the exact hour when Alexander died. But all in all, if a single 60-minute period starting at the top of the hour is desirable, then 3:00–4:00 p.m. seems supported by a better rationale than my earlier proposal of 4:00–5:00 p.m.

9. From Arridaios to Alexander IV (317)

Essence of the Update.—Two kinds of update are presented. First, only recently has it become possible to point to a specific day as the most likely day on which Arridaios died. That day is 26 Dec 317 B.C.E. Second, it is now becoming comprehensively clear how Philip's regnal years were counted and how they relate to those of his successors Antigonos the One-Eyed and Alexander IV, the last two rulers that bear any kind of relationship to the Achaemenid empire as a whole, and how in turn the ways in which years were counted can be correlated with concurrent historical events. [See also Appendix II.]

9.1. A Traditional Day-exact Date for the Death of Arridaios

A probable day-exact date for the death of Arridaios has now emerged. In tablet BM 32238 listing lunar eclipses and lunar eclipse possibilities, one finds the following fragmentary statement at Rev.´ V´ 12´ (Hunger 2001: 6–7): GAN *ina* 27 *Pi-il-l*[*i*?- ....] "Month 9, on Day 27, Pill[i-....]." Owing to the astronomical nature of the text, there is no doubt about the Julian day in question. It is the 24-hour period that lasted from the evening of 25 Dec 317 B.C.E. to the evening of 26 Dec 317 B.C.E.

As Hunger (2001: 8) observes, "this could be a reference to the death of Philip Arrhidaeus," while acknowledging that "[t]he only thing certain (or at least probable) . . . is that Philip is mentioned here." Absolute certainty is indeed too much to hope for. Then again, there are at least three considerations that make it all but certain that the reference here is to the end of Arridaios' reign, most probably by a statement that he died or was executed as in fact he was.

The first consideration is that this type of text as a rule mentions the ends of reigns explicitly (see the list in §2.4.4). Second, the reference to Philip is followed in the next line by a reference to Year 2 of Antigonos Monophthalmos ("the One-eyed"). Antigonos ruled but never officially became king. What else could have been mentioned before the beginning of a reign than the end of the previous one? Only four months or so separated Day 27 Month 9 of Arridaios' Year 7 from Antigonos' Year 2, as follows.

Since the accession year was abandoned first with Arridaios' reign, the first new year of a reign was no longer the beginning of Year 1 but the beginning of Year 2. It is now otherwise also certain, as had been widely but not generally assumed before, that Antigonos' Babylonian Year 2 began with the Babylonian new year in the spring of 316 B.C.E. (Boiy 2001). Accordingly, his Year 1 covers the latter part of a Babylonian calendar year from Arridaios' death on Month 9 Day 27 to the day before new year, that is, four months and a couple of days, there having been a Month 13 (second Addaru) at the end of Year 1. Arridaios died in his Babylonian Year 7, even if tablets are dated to his reign into his Year 8 (*PD* 20).

The third consideration is that Egyptian documents cease being dated to his reign shortly after the presumed reference to his death in BM 32238 (Skeat 1969: 27; Pestman 1967: 10–13). The last document, the Demotic Papyrus Bibliothèque nationale 219 is dated to Month 3 of his Egyptian Year 8, that is, 9 Jan–7 Feb 316 B.C.E., which would be to the weeks following his death. The earliest date for Alexander IV is 10 Apr 316 B.C.E. in the Demotic Papyrus Loeb 27.

In sum, it is reasonable to assume that the reference to Arridaios in BM 32238 is a reference to his death. But the historical method being what it is, I would style the date as the *traditional* date of his death. It is what Babylonian scribes wanted to transmit to posterity as being the date on which he died. It is part of the historical method to examine the gap that may exist between the sources pertaining to an event and the event itself. Babylonian astronomical texts are extremely reliable. When it comes to reports of celestial events, there is hardly any gap between event and source because the events were observed right there and then in Babylon. The same cannot be said about reports of historical events. In the case of Arridaios' death, there is a large gap in space, and hence also in time, between source and event because Arridaios was put to death in Greece. There is no way of knowing how exactly the event was dated in Greece. Nor are the circumstances known in which the date was transmitted to Babylon and converted. All we can do is to accept the traditional date and be aware that it cannot be excluded that there was a gap between this date and the actual date. Among the Greek authors, Diodorus (XIX 11) gives the most precise number for Arridaios' reign, namely six years and four months. Accordingly, since Arridaios' first day of reign was 12 Jun 323 B.C.E., he would have died in about October, on a date that falls only two months before the traditional Babylonian date.

Arridaios was held prisoner in a tiny cell and the bare necessities were passed to him through a small opening (Diodoros XI 11,4). His end came when his mother Olympias τὸν μὲν Φίλιππον προσέταξε Θραξί τισιν ἐκκεντῆσαι "ordered some Thracians to stab Philip to death" (Diodoros XI 11,5). Day 27 Month 9 of Arridaios' Year 7 lasts from the evening of 25 Dec 317 B.C.E. to the evening of 26 Dec 317 B.C.E. Is it possible to eliminate either 25 or December 26 or at least opt for one as being more probable than the other? I believe that 26 December is the preferable option, in light of the following consideration.

When Arridaios died in Greece, his death was associated with a certain day number. There are two possibilities. He died during daylight or he did not. But with either possibility, the day number would be the same.

If he did not die during daylight, it seems unlikely that the guards would have gone to bed and risen at night to commit the act. Arridaios was a prisoner and had nowhere to go. He did not need to be surprised in the middle of the night. Therefore, if Arridaios was not killed during daylight, it is still possible that he was killed in the time preceding sunrise or following sunset. Activities undertaken at both those times are continuous with activities undertaken in the daylight period between them. For most people in antiquity, days were periods of light counted in succession and separated from one another by uncounted episodes of darkness called night. Any activity before dawn and after sunset would typically form an organic whole with any activity undertaken during the contiguous daylight period and therefore be assigned the same day number as the daylight period that it abutted. One hardly imagines anyone in daily life changing the day number at sunrise or sunset in the middle of a single sequence of connected activities.

What is more, there are many other reasons to assume that, in Greece and Macedonia, an evening would share the same day number with the daylight period immediately preceding it. I would hope to treat this essential point in more detail elsewhere (see, already, Bilfinger's profound study [1888]).

From Greece, a certain month and day date associated with Arridaios' death reached Babylon and was converted somehow into a Babylonian day number. In choosing a Babylonian day number, the focus would be on daylight. If Arridaios had died in the evening, it would be the evening *following* the daylight in question because the day number is Greek in origin. That would in fact mean that he had died on Babylonian Month 9 Day *28*. In Babylonian astronomical texts, the day rigorously begins in the evening. But it is to be doubted that the same practice was followed in daily life. In modern times, the Sabbath and Jewish and Muslim festivals begin in the evening. But no one invited to a meeting taking place in the evening of the fourth day of the week will come in the evening that immediately follows daylight of the third day.

There is the following improbable scenario: (1) Arridaios died in the evening; (2) Babylonian scribes knew this; (3) they were aware that the day began in the morning in Greece; and (4) they knew the exact correlation between the Macedonian and the Babylonian calendars. If so, they would have needed to *change* the number and depart from the procedure that was followed in converting dates of daylight events. If they normally converted the day date of a daylight event from x to y, they would have had to converted the day date of an evening event from x to $y + 1$. Accordingly, they would have dated the event correctly and Arridaios would have died in the evening of 25 December.

However, one hesitates to assume such complexity. It is more likely that the report of a day number x arrived from Greece and that the daylight period of that day was associated with the daylight period of a Babylonian day y. If the event had occurred in the evening, then the date would be Babylonian Day $y + 1$ of the astronomical texts. But since Julian 26 December runs from midnight to midnight, the date in either case would be 26 December.

So far, the possible difference in the Macedonian and Babylonian day counts has not been taken into account. Both are lunar and could not have been far apart. Then again, Babylonian astronomical texts date the battle of Gaugamela of 1 Oct 331 B.C.E. to Day 24 of Ululu (Sachs and Hunger 1988: 178-179) and Plutarch (*Life of Camillus,* 19,5) dates it to Day 26 of Boedromion. There are indications that the Macedonian lunar month began one or two days before the lunar month of Babylonian astronomical texts. But this topic exceeds the present investigation and I hope to treat it elsewhere. Could Babylonian scribes have known of this correlation and made the conversion correctly? In the end, we cannot be certain. If there are any places where one might hope to find the needed sophisticated understanding of the differences between the two calendars, it would be the royal chancellery of the Macedonian-Achaemenid empire and the scribes of Babylonian astronomical texts.

In sum, Month 9 Day 27 lasts from evening 25 December to evening 26 December in 317 B.C.E. But if Month 9 Day 27 is correct day and Arridaios happened to have died in the evening in Greece, that evening would rather have been the one of 26 Dec 317 B.C.E. His traditional Babylonian date of death can therefore be converted into Julian 26 Dec 317 B.C.E.

9.2. Regnal Year Counts in Egypt and Babylon in the Wake of Arridaios' Death down to 304 B.C.E. and Their Relation to Political History

9.2.1. Counting Years in Daily Life and in Astronomy

In a second update, it is now possible to present a comprehensive survey of how years were dated from Arridaios' death in late 317 B.C.E. onward, down to the time when the final faint traces of the Achaemenid empire vanished in 304 B.C.E. I expect most if not all of the survey presented below to withstand the test of time. But the need for minor adjustments cannot be excluded. Meanwhile, presenting a comprehensive picture, which does not now exist, may add clarity to the study of the subject. The survey pertains to how years were counted in daily life, not in specialized contexts such as astronomy. Regnal year counting in astronomical texts such as the Babylonian Solar Saros and Lunar Saros Canon (see now Aaboe and others 1991) and in astronomical tools of time-reckoning such as Ptolemy's Royal Canon (Depuydt 1995d) is partly artificial. For one, all reigns are counted in full calendar years, whereas rulers in actual fact can ascend to the throne on any day of the year. Still, the dating of astronomical texts overlaps mostly with that of daily life and therefore contributes to lending solidity to the following account. All details pertaining to past research and sources cannot be repeated here. Even so, the sparse references should indirectly lead to all relevant sources and studies.

What did scribes in Egypt and Mesopotamia do when Arridaios died?

9.2.2. Egypt

The case of Egypt is simple (for details, see Skeat 1969: 27-28; Pestman 1967: 10-13). Scribes simply counted by Alexander IV until Ptolemy I became king.

At the latest by 10 Apr 316 B.C.E. (Papyrus Loeb 27), scribes began dating by Alexander IV's Year 1, presumably as soon as they learned in early 316 B.C.E. of Arridaios' death at the end of 317 B.C.E. in his Egyptian Year 8. They continued this count until Ptolemy I fully styled himself as king in 304 B.C.E. Alexander IV's Year 2 began on the Egyptian new year of 10 Nov 316 B.C.E. His Year 13 began on the new year of 7 Nov 305 B.C.E. and lasted at least until 6 Jan-4 Feb 304 (Demotic Papyri Louvre 2427 and 2440). Sometime before new year of 7 Nov 304 B.C.E., Ptolemy I's Year 1 must have begun. His Year 2 definitely did on new year of 7 Nov 304 B.C.E.

Regnal dating obscures the fact that Alexander IV hardly ever ruled in effect. At Arridaios' death, he was still a young child. And sometime in 311-309 B.C.E., just as his coming of age could threaten any *de facto* rulers, he was put to death along with his mother Roxane. Still, documents were dated to his reign for five to six more years or so after his death. Ptolemy, the later Ptolemy (I) Soter, in actual fact ruled Egypt from soon after Alexander the Great's death. He would later, in Greek manuscripts, count his regnal years from that early. Ptolemy's practice of years of reign according to Alexander IV coincides with his styling himself as governor rather than as king. The two complement one another.

9.2.3. Babylon

9.2.3.1. Principal Characteristic

The case of Babylon is not as simple as that of Egypt (see now Boiy 2000, 2001, and 2002b). The difference with Egypt is that authority over Memphis was never challenged whereas political control over Babylon was. At Babylon, the principal contenders were Antigonos Monophthalmos and Seleukos. Accordingly, regnal year counting at Babylon in the wake of Arridaios' death exhibits a peculiar pattern. In 316-15 B.C.E., years were counted by Alexander IV only, in 315-311 B.C.E. by Antigonos (perhaps on occasion jointly with Alexander IV), in 311-304 B.C.E. again by Alexander IV only, and finally from 304 B.C.E. according to Seleukos I.

The seeming complexity of this pattern can be much reduced by telescoping it into a single main distinctive property. By that property, regnal year counting followed exactly the same pattern as in Egypt except for a period of interference by Antigonos. If Antigonos had never challenged Seleukos, the Babylonian and Egyptian counts of reigns would have been the same, with one exception. Egyptian scribes began counting by Alexander IV at Philip's death itself, whereas Babylonian scribes waited for several months to do so, perhaps because Alexander IV was so very young. After some time they did anyway. The similarity in the year counts in Egypt and Babylon, initially at least, reflects the political history of the times. Ptolemy and Seleukos, who instituted the year counts, were otherwise in every way sympathetic to one another. When Seleukos was in trouble in 315 B.C.E., he fled to Ptolemy in Egypt. The two fought alongside one another in the ensuing Third War of the Diadochi. Both refused to style themselves as king, even after Alexander IV's death sometime in 311-309 B.C.E. When they finally did in 304 B.C.E., they did so in synchrony.

The course of events may now be reviewed in more detail from a chronological perspective, while correlating chronological history with political history. Then again, the complexities concerning the wars of the Successors of Alexander cannot all be addressed here.

9.2.3.2. 317 B.C.E.-315 B.C.E.: Arridaios, post-Arridaios, and early Alexander IV

At Babylon, Arridaios' reign ended on Month 9 Day 27 of his Babylonian Year 7, that is, 25/26 (evening to evening) Dec 317 B.C.E. Presumably, he died on that day or not long before. But documents kept being dated by him after his death for at least another 10 to 11 months, until at least Month 7 Day 19 of his Year 8, that is, *ca.* 9 Oct 316 B.C.E. (tablet BM 79012 [Boiy 2000: 118 note 15, 119]).

What happened next is not entirely clear. But there are strong indications that it was decided to begin dating according to the very young Alexander IV, Alexander the Great's son, who was six or so at the time. Documents dating to Alexander's Years 1 and 2 have survived. Then there is a gap in the documentation until Year 6. One exception is a document dated to Year 4 discussed below. The tablets dated to Alexander IV's Years 1 and 2 (BM 78948 and *CT* 49 13) could easily be fitted in the period between the last tablet dated to Arridaios of *ca.* 9 Oct 316 B.C.E. and the first tablet dated to Antigonos (*CT* 49 34) of Month 9 of his Year 3, that is, *ca.* 12 Dec 315 B.C.E.-*ca.* 6 Jan 314 B.C.E. (so Boiy 2000: 119). It is difficult to see how else these tablets can be interpreted than by assuming that documents began to be dated by Alexander IV as soon as dating by Arridaios ceased. Dating by Alexander IV lasted about a year, perhaps a little more or a little less. This period overlapped with two Babylonian years, the first beginning on *ca.* 28 Apr 316 B.C.E. and the second beginning on *ca.* 16 Apr 315 B.C.E.

9.2.3.3. 317 B.C.E.–308 B.C.E.: Antigonos

Nine Babylonian regnal years of Antigonos are attested in the surviving documents (for comprehensive tabulations of regnal years in the early Hellenistic period, from 331/30 or 330/329 to 301/300, see Boiy 2000: 121 and 2002b: 254). These regnal years overlap with the nine Babylonian calendar years in the period lasting from new year in the spring of 317 B.C.E. to new year in the spring of 308 B.C.E. In no case does a single calendar year coincide with two different regnal year numbers. In that sense, the sources present a coherent picture. All confirm one another. In the case of Alexander the Great, there was more than one way of designating years by ordinal numbers (see §7 above). In the case of Antigonos, there was only one. Yet, at least four different ways of counting are attested. The differences pertain to where the count begins and where it ends. Not all counts begin with Year 1 and not all counts end with Year 9.

There are four ways of counting Antigonos' years. They are characterized by four different beginnings and two different ends. The counts can begin as late as with the beginning of Year 3 and end as late as with the end of Year 9. The political history of the time easily accounts for differences at the beginning and end of the count. Antigonos was firmly in control of Babylon for only four years of the nine years for which dates of his reign have survived. It is in those years that the so-called Third Diadoch War was waged pitting Ptolemy and Seleukos against Antigonos (cf. Wheatley 1998). This period of about four years lasts from about summer 315 B.C.E., when Seleukos fled to Egypt, to some time in 311 B.C.E., probably around May 311 B.C.E., when Seleukos reconquered Babylon. At the beginning of this period, Antigonos was in his Year 3; at the end, in his Year 7.

First, as regards the beginning of Antigonos' reign in terms of surviving year counts, there are four different year counts and each has its own beginning. Evidently, only one corresponds to the actual beginning of the reign. The four beginnings are as follows: (1) new year in the spring of 317 B.C.E. (when he did not yet rule Babylon) as the schematic beginning of Year 1 in certain astronomical texts; (2) the death of Arridaios on 25/26 Dec 317 B.C.E. (when he did not yet rule Babylon) as backdated beginning of his reign, also used in certain other astronomical texts; (3) new year in the spring of 315 B.C.E. (when he did not yet rule Babylon) as beginning of Year 3 and backdated beginning of the year count in yet other astronomical texts; (4) the actual beginning of his reign in Babylon, that is, at least by the date of the earliest dated tablet, namely *CT* 49 34, dated to Month 9 of Year 3, that is, *ca.* 12 Dec 315 B.C.E.–*ca.* 6 Jan 314 B.C.E. (Boiy 2000: 119), but possibly as early as summer 315 B.C.E.

The following events account for these four beginnings. Certainly by late 315 B.C.E., and probably earlier, scribes ceased dating years by Alexander IV and began dating years by Antigonos. The change can obviously be correlated to Antigonos' rise in power and Seleukos' flight to Egypt around mid-315 B.C.E. (Diodoros XIX 55–56,1 [cf. Hölbl 1994: 18]). Neither Seleukos nor Ptolemy nor Antigonos claimed the title of king. But unlike Seleukos and Ptolemy, Antigonos did count his regnal years in Babylon from the death of Arridaios. The short period that had been dated in actuality to Alexander IV was thus obliterated at least conceptually. It is easy to understand why Antigonos would have wanted to expunge a year count instituted by his adversary Seleukos. Consequently, his year count is one higher than Alexander IV's (see below). Antigonos' Year 3 fully overlaps with Alexander IV's Year 2, and so on.

It is possible that Antigonos dated the four years of his sole rule over Babylon on occasion both to Alexander IV and himself. Boiy (2000: 120) reconstructs a double date "Year 4, which is (*šá ši-i*) [Year 5(?)] of Antigonos" in *AION Suppl.* 77 87, lines 19–20. Alexander IV is not mentioned, but it is difficult to see with which other ruler Antigonos would jointly date his reign.

The four months and a few days from Arridaios' death to the end of the Babylonian calendar year on *ca.* 27 Mar 316 B.C.E. became Antigonos' virtual Year 1. The calendar year lasting from new year in the spring of 316 B.C.E. to new year in the spring of 315 B.C.E. became his virtual Year 2. The virtual part of his Year 3 began on new year in the spring of 315 B.C.E. In the summer of 315 B.C.E., Antigonos conquered Babylon and his actual reign over Babylon began, styled as Year 3. This is one of the four ways in which his years were counted. This beginning is independent of human choice. It is a fact of history. By contrast, the three other beginnings are the result of decisions by human beings. They are therefore virtual and not actual. One beginning must have been the outcome of a decision by Antigonos. It is Arridaios' death at the end of 317 B.C.E. This virtual beginning is probably used in BM 32238 listing lunar eclipses and lunar eclipse possibilities (see §9.1). Arridaios' Year 7 is followed by Antigonos' Year 2. It is not clear how the four months or so from Arridaios' death to the beginning of Antigonos' Year 2 are designated. In fact, they did not need to be: the text lists events at six or five month intervals. If the entire calendar year was conceived as Antigonos' Year 1, BM 32238 would evidence a fifth manner of year counting.

The two other virtual year counts also result from decisions by astronomers. They appear in Babylonian astronomical texts of the theoretical kind. Astronomical texts of the observational kind follow the calendar of daily life, as one might expect. In the Solar Saros, the count begins with Year 3 on new year in the spring of 315 B.C.E. (Boiy 2001, 2002b). In other words, the actual beginning of Antigonos' reign is backdated to the beginning of the calendar year. Year 3 is preceded by Arridaios' Years 7 and 8, both full calendar years. In the Saros (Lunar) Canon, the count begins with Year 1 on new year in the spring of 317 B.C.E. (Boiy 2000: 116). In this case, the virtual beginning of Antigonos' reign at Arridaios' death is backdated. The Saros Canon's Years 1 and 2 are the same as Arridaios' Years 7 and 8 of the Solar Saros.

Each count bears an indirect relationship to a different historical reality. The Solar Saros reflects the fact that Antigonos did not rule Babylon before mid-315 B.C.E. The Saros Canon reflects the fact that Antigonos himself backdated his reign to late 317 B.C.E.

As regards the end of Antigonos' reign, the four year counts exhibit two different endings and *neither* corresponds to the actual end of Antigonos' full and undivided control over Babylon some time in 311 B.C.E., apparently around May (see below), when Seleukos conquered Babylon. One ending falls before that time and the other after it. The ending that falls before it is found in theoretical astronomical texts. Both the Solar Saros and the Saros Canon end with the end of Year 6 as both a regnal and a calendar year. Antigonos' Year 6 is the Babylonian calendar year lasting from 13 Apr 312 B.C.E. to 2 Apr 311 B.C.E. This ending presumably bears an indirect relationship to the end of Antigonos' firm control, which may have been recorded in astronomical texts of the observational kind. The ending that falls later and extends to Year 9 is found in business documents: *CT* 49 50 is dated to Year 7, *TBER* 88 (AO 26765) to Year 8, and BM 105211 to Year 9 (Boiy 2000: 119). The later ending serves as evidence of the struggle for Babylon between Seleukos and Antigonos and its surroundings in the wake of Seleukos' reconquest of the city (for details, see Wheatley 2002).

9.2.3.4. Antigonos' Years in Cuneiform Sources: Survey

new year in spring 317	Backdated schematic Year **1** begins in Saros Canon. Arridaios' Year 7 begins in Solar Saros.
25/26 Dec 317	Backdated virtual regnal Year **1** begins when Arridaios dies in his Year 7.
new year in spring 316	Arridaios' posthumous Year 8 begins in Solar Saros and in the calendar of daily life. Backdated schematic Year **2** begins in Saros Canon and lunar eclipse tablet BM 32238. Backdated virtual regnal Year **2** begins.
later in calendar year 317/16	Arridaios' posthumous Year 8 ends and Alexander IV's Year 1 begins in calendar of daily life.
new year in spring 315	Backdated schematic Year **3** begins in Saros Canon and Solar Saros. Backdated virtual regnal Year **3** begins. Alexander IV's actual regnal Year 2 begins.

later in	Actual Year **3** of uncontested rule over Babylon begins as Alexander IV's Year 2
calendar year 316/315	ends.
new year in spring 314	Year **4** of Babylonian rule begins.
new year in spring 313	Year **5** of Babylonian rule begins.
new year in spring 312	Year **6** of Babylonian rule begins.
new year in spring 311	Year **7** of Babylonian rule begins.
about May 311	Uncontested rule over Babylon ends.
	Alexander IV's year count resumes with Year 6.
new year in spring 310	Alexander IV's Year 7 begins.
calendar year 311/310	Year **7** attested.
sometime in 311–309	Alexander IV is put to death.
new year in spring 309	Alexander IV's Year 8, posthumous or actual, begins.
calendar year 310/309	Year **8** attested.
calendar year 309/308	Year **9** attested.

9.2.3.5. 311 B.C.E.–304 B.C.E.: The Later Alexander IV and Seleukos

When Seleukos reconquered Babylon some time in 311 B.C.E., Antigonos' Year 7 was underway. Seleukos resumed the count according to Alexander IV that he had used when ruling Babylon in 317 B.C.E.–315 B.C.E. The earliest known tablet dated again to Alexander IV is BM 22022, whose date is Month 2 Day 10/19 of his Year 6, that is, *ca.* 11/20 May 311 B.C.E. (Boiy 2000: 119 note 19). It may be inferred that Seleukos was again considered ruler of Babylon from around that time, possible a little earlier but probably from after new year or Month 1 Day 1 (see below).

By the time Seleukos arrived in Babylon, the count according to Alexander IV was in its Year 6 , not its Year 7. Consequently, the early days of the calendar year lasting from spring 311 B.C.E. to spring 310 B.C.E. must have been Year 7 of Antigonos if Seleukos conquered Babylon after new year and the rest of that same calendar year was Year 6 of Alexander IV. Year 7 of Alexander IV began on the Babylonian new year in the spring of 310 B.C.E., one year after Antigonos' Year 7 if he had had a Year 7.

After Alexander IV was put to death sometime in 311–309 B.C.E., Seleukos kept dating by him posthumously until at least some time in Alexander IV's Year 11 (Boiy 2002b: 249). Year 11 began in the spring of 306 B.C.E. The earliest attested date according to Seleukos is found in BM 78603 or *CT* 4 plate 29*d* (McEwan 1985; Boiy 2000: 120 with note 25). It falls two days after new year in the spring of 304 B.C.E., namely on Month 1 Day 3 Year 8, that is, *ca.* 16 Apr 304 B.C.E.

When Seleukos began dating years in his own name, new year in the spring of 304 B.C.E. did not become the beginning of his Year 1 but of his Year 8. In other words, the calendar year lasting from new year in the spring of 311 B.C.E. to new year in the spring of 310 B.C.E. came to be counted as his Year 1, presumably because it was in that year that he had reconquered Babylon. Indeed, the fact that Year 8 begins in the spring of 304 B.C.E. serves as an argument in favor of the notion that Seleukos reconquered Babylon after and not before new year in the spring of 311 B.C.E. If he had conquered Babylon before new year, the time up to new year might have been counted as his Year 1. The accession year had been abandoned beginning with Arridaios' reign in 323 B.C.E. It is to the schematic beginning of new year in the spring of 311 B.C.E. that the King List from Uruk (*BaM Beih.* II, 88 [Boiy 2000: 116, 121]) by implication refers when it gives Seleukos 31 years, following Alexander III's seven, Arridaios' six, and Antigonos' six.

In which calendar year did Seleukos abandon the year count according to Alexander IV and began counting by his own years, backdating the beginning to new year in the spring of 311 B.C.E.? The earliest surviving dated tablet, BM 78603, is dated to the third month of his Year 8. But there are indications that he may have begun his own count with his Year 7 in the preceding calendar year lasting from spring 305 B.C.E. to spring 304 B.C.E., it is not known when. No tablets are attested from Year 7 (Boiy 2002b: 249). However, the Solar Canon's schematic count and the King List from Babylon (*Iraq* 16, plate 53 [Boiy 2000: 116–17, 121]) begin with Year 7. The King List explicitly equates Year 7 from spring 311 B.C.E. with Year 1 of Seleukos (McEwan 1985: 169 note 1). This fact may indirectly reflect a historical reality, namely that

Seleukos had begun counting with what he styled as his Year 7, beginning with new year in the spring of 311 B.C.E. Alexander IV's Year 11 would then span the entire calendar year lasting from spring 306 B.C.E. to spring 305 B.C.E. If Seleukos did not begin his own count on new year in the spring of 305 B.C.E., then Alexander IV would have had a Year 12, which is not attested.

After Seleukos' death, the count according to his reign starting with new year in the spring of 311 B.C.E. as the beginning of Year 1 continued. Thus, the regnal year count was transformed into an era. An era is a count of years in perpetuity beginning from a certain starting-point. The so-called Seleucid era is the earliest era in history. Strictly speaking, the era only begins at Seleukos' death on *ca.* 24 Sep 281 B.C.E. (*PD* 21).

The Saros Lunar Canon begins counting by Seleukos with his Year 1 from 311 B.C.E. Alexander's Years 6–11 of the Solar Saros are the same as Seleukos' Years 1–6 of Saros Canon. These six years constitute the six-year period that the King List from Babylon (*Iraq* 16, plate 53) assigns to Alexander IV.

The Syrian-Macedonian version of the Seleucid era begins in the fall of 312 B.C.E. because the Macedonian year begins in the fall. Kugler (1922) established that the Seleucid Era of 1 Maccabees began a whole year earlier on the Babylonian new year in the spring of 312 B.C.E. Accordingly, there are three attested beginnings for the Seleucid era.

10. How Did They Die?

Thirteen kings ruled the Achaemenid empire. The first ten were Achaemenids. The last ten are discussed above. In the following list, the length of reign is represented by the round number of 365-day Egyptian years found in Ptolemy's Royal Canon: Cyrus (9 years), Cambyses (8), Darius I (36), Xerxes I (21), Artaxerxes I (41), Darius II (19), Artaxerxes II (46), Artaxerxes III (21), Arses (2), Darius III (4), Alexander III "the Great" (8), Arridaios (7), Alexander IV (12). No historical event is more important, somewhat anticlimactically, than the death of a ruler. Surveying the manner in which the thirteen kings died may be useful (cf. Briant 2002 [1996]: 772–73).

It is not altogether uncharacteristic of antiquity that many rulers of the Achaemenid empire met a violent death, at least six and possibly as many as eight out of thirteen. Regnal successions were not regulated by law. Accordingly, violence was often unavoidable. The ways in which the kings died bears some connection to the rise and fall of the empire as an organic entity.

Six of thirteen rulers, or about half, were killed. Four were murdered: (no. 4) Xerxes I; (no. 8) Artaxerxes III; (no. 9) Arses; and (no. 10) Darius III. Two were executed: (no. 12) Arridaios and (no. 13) Alexander IV. It seems indicative of the growing instability of the Achaemenid empire in its final decades that five of its last six kings were killed. In fact, the ways in which these five were killed exhibits a certain progression towards a climax of its own as the deaths become less and less dignified. Nos. 8 and 9, Artaxerxes III and Arses, were assassinated by a powerful courtier. No. 10's, Darius III's, was less stately, as he was stabbed while fleeing after losing his empire at Gaugamela. And the last two, nos. 12 and 13, Arridaios and Alexander IV, were killed off rather unceremoniously while in confinement. Only Xerxes I was murdered by a member of his own family, a son (§1). The empire was still in its heyday at the time. Some ephemeral rulers and pretenders were also killed, including Bardiya in 522, Xerxes II in 424, Sekyndianos in 424, and Cyrus the Younger in 401. But then, it is often this very fate that marks a ruler as ephemeral.

Two more rulers, (no. 1) Cyrus and (no. 2) Cambyses, possibly also met a violent death. The way in which they may have died is again in a way symbolic of the evolution of the empire. They who made Persia into an empire by the conquests of Babylon (539) and Egypt (527–25) may have met their death while on expedition to conquer new lands. Cyrus perhaps died in battle and Cambyses perhaps died in Syria by accident or suicide. They were followed by Darius I and Xerxes I who failed to subdue Greece. Things took a turn with Artaxerxes I, who seems to have been more peace-loving and generous. But it would last another century before Greece got back at Persia.

Of the five remaining rulers, two are known to have died of illness—both having contracted their disease in the city of Babylon as it happens—namely (no. 6) Darius II and (no. 11) Alexander the Great.

Three rulers remain, namely (no. 3) Darius I, (no. 5) Artaxerxes I), and (no. 7) Artaxerxes II. The manner of death is not detailed in any source. But it is probably no coincidence that these are the three rulers that reigned by far the longest: Darius I for about 36 years, Artaxerxes I for about 41 years, and Artaxerxes II for about 46 years. Together, these three rulers account for about 60% of the total length of the Achaemenid dynasty (539–331). Only Xerxes I, Darius II, and Artaxerxes III come close in length of reign, with around 20 years each. Their reigns were cut short when two of them were murdered and the third contracted a deadly disease. None of the other rulers reigned more than 10 years.

The most obvious solution is that Darius I, Artaxerxes I, and Artaxerxes II died of old age or, to use an equivalent expression, of natural causes. Everyone dies of something. But dying of old age implies that what one dies of does not matter because one is expected to die anyhow. If one had not died of one thing, one would soon have died of another anyhow. By contrast, the cause of death is significant for those who die younger because it produces something unexpected. About only one of the three deaths has a statement survived, namely Darius I's. Briant (2002 [1996]: 518) writes:

"Upon returning to Persia, Darius offered sacrifices and died. . . The throne passed to his son Xerxes." With these simple words, Ctesias, or at least Photius, treats the succession of Darius (§§19–20)—leaving the historian grasping at straws.

The impression is that of a candle being extinguished. That impression quite possibly concords with historical fact.

11. FINAL REGNAL YEARS OF THE ACHAEMENID EMPIRE: TABULATION

A comprehensive tabulation of all the regnal years of the Achaemenid empire from 539 B.C.E. to 304 B.C.E. in both Egypt and Babylon would be a convenient tool, listing the Julian equivalents of all the new years in both calendars. Such a tool exceeds the scope of the present paper. What is presented instead below is a tabulation of the years 340 B.C.E.–304 B.C.E. (for two tabulations of the attested systems of regnal year dating in Babylon converted to whole calendar years from 331–330 B.C.E. to 304 B.C.E., see Boiy 2000: 121 and 2002b: 254). Only recently has a comprehensive survey of the regnal years in this period become possible. Meanwhile, pending a more comprehensive tool, other tabulations are available for earlier years. *PD* is still the main tool for regnal years in Babylon, even if a list of all the beginnings of months of which the exact Julian date is known remains desirable, as was noted at the outset of this paper. Tabulations of the regnal years of Achaemenid rulers in Egypt are found in Depuydt 2006a: 276–83. Earlier versions appeared in id. 1995b: 168–71, as well as in id. 1996: 189–90 (Cambyses only) and in id. 1995d: 108–112 (Ptolemy's Royal Canon). Errata to these tables are included in the lists of errata presented in the appendix to this table.

The Julian equivalents of the beginnings of Egyptian regnal years are day-exact, that is, certain to the exact day. The Julian equivalents of the beginnings of Babylonian regnal years may be off by a day. In some cases, the Julian dates are day-exact because the beginning of the year can be placed on the exact day owing to information found in Babylonian astronomical texts. On the basis of information derived from the astronomical Diaries (Sachs and Hunger 1988), five New Year's Days are day-exact in 340 B.C.E.–304 B.C.E.: those falling on 12 Apr 339 B.C.E., 7 Apr 325 B.C.E., 14 Apr 323 B.C.E., 4 Apr 322 B.C.E., and 10 Apr 309 B.C.E. Additional detail for each is provided in the table below. It is possible that other new years can be made day-exact on the basis of information derived from other astronomical texts. The Julian dates of the 32 other New Year's Days in the period 340 B.C.E.–304 B.C.E. in the table below are those of *PD* 35–37. They "have been calculated by the new-moon tables of Karl Schoch" (*PD* 25). In 11 of the 37 dates, or about 30%, the Julian day date in Sidersky's table of equivalences (1916: 48–50) falls a day later than the date in *PD*, namely the Babylonian new years of 338 B.C.E. (2, not 1, April), 337 B.C.E. (20, not 19, April), 328 B.C.E. (11, not 10, April), 319 B.C.E. (2, not 1, April), 318 B.C.E. (21, not 20, April), 317 B.C.E. (9, not 8, April), 316 B.C.E. (29, not 28, March), 315 B.C.E. 17, not 16, April), 308 B.C.E. (31, not 30, March), 305 B.C.E. (27, not 26, March), and 304 B.C.E. (15, not 14, April).

Regnal Years in Egypt and in Babylon in 340 B.C.E.–304 B.C.E.

[Egyptian and Babylonian new years are in **bold**, Egyptian years containing a 29 February are in *italics*.]

Era of Nabo-nassar	Egyptian Regnal Year	Length of 365-day Egyptian year (Julian dates other than new year derived from lunar dates may be 1 or 2 days off)	Length of Year in Babylon having been derived from lunar dates, these Julian dates may be 1 or 2 days off)	Babylonian Regnal Year
(409	Nectanebo II 20	**16 Nov 340** – ? [a])	**22 Apr 340** – 11 Apr 339	Artaxerxes III 19
410	Artaxerxes III 21	**16 Nov 339** – a day in 27 Aug–25 Sep 338 [c]	**12 Apr 339** [b] – 31 Mar 338	Artaxerxes III 20
410	Arses dated how? [d]	a day in 27 Aug–25 Sep 338 [c] – 15 Nov 338	**1 Apr 338** – a day in 27 Aug–25 Sep 338 [c]	Artaxerxes III 21
411	*Arses 1*	*16 Nov 338* [e] *– 14 Nov 337*	a day in 27 Aug–25 Sep 338 [c] – 18 Apr 337	Arses accession year
412	Arses 2	**15 Nov 337** – 14 Nov 336	**19 Apr 337** – 8 Apr 336	Arses 1
412	Darius III dated how? [d]	a day in *ca.* Sep 336–18 Mar 335 [f] – 14 Nov 336	**9 Apr 336** – a day in *ca.* Sep 336–18 Mar 335 [f]	Arses 2
413	Darius III 1	**15 Nov 336** [g] – 14 Nov 335	a day in *ca.* Sep 336–18 Mar 335 [f] – 28 Mar 335	Darius III accession year
414	Darius III 2	**15 Nov 335** – 14 Nov 334	**29 Mar 335** – 16 Apr 334	Darius III 1
415	*Darius III 3*	*15 Nov 334 – 13 Nov 333*	**17 Apr 334** – 4 Apr 333	Darius III 2
416	Darius III 4	**14 Nov 333** – Nov/Dec 332 [h]	**5 Apr 333** – 24 Mar 332	Darius III 3
417	Darius III 5? [i] Or Alexander III 1? [h]	**14 Nov 332** [j] – Nov/Dec 332 [h]	**25 Mar 332** – 12 Apr 331	Darius III 4

64

Era of Nabo-nassar	Egyptian Regnal Year	Length of 365-day Egyptian year (Julian dates other than new year derived from lunar dates may be 1 or 2 days off)	Length of Year in Babylon (having been derived from lunar dates, these Julian dates may be 1 or 2 days off)	Babylonian Regnal Year	
417	Alexander III 1	Nov/Dec 332[h] – 13 Nov 331	13 Apr 331 – 1 Oct 331[k]	Darius III 5	
			Oct 331[k] – 2 Apr 330	Alexander III accession year[l]	
418	Alexander III 2	14 Nov 331 – 13 Nov 330	3 Apr 330[m] – 20 Apr 329	Alexander III 7	(Saros: 1)
419	*Alexander III 3*	*14 Nov 330 – 12 Nov 329*	21 Apr 329 – 9 Apr 328	Alexander III 8	(Saros: 2)
420	Alexander III 4	13 Nov 329 – 12 Nov 328	10 Apr 328 – 30 Mar 327	Alexander III 9	(Saros: 3)
421	Alexander III 5	13 Nov 328 – 12 Nov 327	31 Mar 327 – 18 Apr 326	Alexander III 10	(Saros: 4)
422	Alexander III 6	13 Nov 327 – 12 Nov 326	19 Apr 326 – 6 Apr 325	Alexander III 11	(Saros: 5)
423	*Alexander III 7*	*13 Nov 326 – 11 Nov 325*	7 Apr 325[n] – 26 Mar 324	Alexander III 12	(Saros: 6)
424	Alexander III 8	12 Nov 325 – 11 Nov 324	27 Mar 324 – 14 Apr 323	Alexander III 13	(Saros: 7)
425	Alexander III 9	12 Nov 324[o] – 11 Jun 323[p]	14 Apr 323[q] – 11 Jun 323[p]	Alexander III 14	(Saros: Philip 1)
425	Philip Arridaios 1	12 Jun 323 – 11 Nov 323	12 Jun 323 – 3 Apr 323	Arridaios 1	(Saros: same)
426	Arridaios 2	12 Nov 323 – 11 Nov 322	4 Apr 322[r] – 21 Apr 321	Arridaios 2	(Saros: same)
427	*Arridaios 3*	*12 Nov 322 – 10 Nov 321*	22 Apr 321 – 11 Apr 320	Arridaios 3	(Saros: same)
428	Arridaios 4	11 Nov 321 – 10 Nov 320	12 Apr 320 – 31 Mar 319	Arridaios 4	(Saros: same)

Updates to Achaemenid Chronology

Era of Nabo-nassar	Egyptian Regnal Year	Length of 365-day Egyptian year (some Julian dates other than new year derived from lunar dates, from lunar dates may be 1 or 2 days off)	Length of Year in Babylon (having been derived from lunar dates, these Julian dates may be 1 or 2 days off)	Babylonian Regnal Year
429	Arridaios 5	11 Nov 320 – 10 Nov 319	**1 Apr 319** – 19 Apr 318	Arridaios 5 (Saros: same)
430	Arridaios 6	11 Nov 319 – 10 Nov 318	**20 Apr 318** – 7 Apr 317	Arridaios 6 (Saros: same)
431	*Arridaios 7*	11 Nov 318 – 9 Nov 317^s	**8 Apr 317**^t – 27 Mar 316^u	Arridaios 7
432	Arridaios 8	10 Nov 317 – no later than 9 Apr 316^v		(Solar Saros: Arridaios 7)
				(Saros Canon: Antigonos 1)
	Alexander IV 1	at the latest by 10 Apr 316^v – 9 Nov 316	**28 Mar 316** – at least until 9 Oct 316^w	Arridaios 8
				(Solar Saros: Arridaios 8)
				(Saros Canon: Antigonos 2)
			no earlier than 10 Oct^w – 15 Apr 315	Alexander IV 1
				(Solar Saros: Arridaios 8)
				(Saros Canon: Antigonos 2)
433	Alexander IV 2	10 Nov 316 – 9 Nov 315	**16 Apr 315**^x – no later than 19 Jul 315^y	Alexander IV 2
				(Both Saros: Antigonos 3)
			at the latest by 20 Jul 315^y – 4 Apr 314	Antigonos 3^z
				(Both Saros: Antigonos 3)
434	Alexander IV 3	10 Nov 315 – 9 Nov 314	**5 Apr 314** – 24 Mar 313	Antigonos 4^z
				(Both Saros: Antigonos 4)

FINAL REGNAL YEARS OF THE ACHAEMENID EMPIRE

Era of Nabo-nassar	Egyptian Regnal Year	Length of 365-day Egyptian year (some Julian dates other than new year derived from lunar dates may be 1 or 2 days off)	Length of Year in Babylon (having been derived from lunar dates, these Julian dates may be 1 or 2 days off)	Babylonian Regnal Year
435	Alexander IV 4	10 Nov 314 – 8 Nov 313	25 Mar 313 – 12 Apr 312	Antigonos 5 [z]
				(Both Saros: Antigonos 5)
436	Alexander IV 5	9 Nov 313 – 8 Nov 312	13 Apr 312 – 2 Apr 311	Antigonos 6 [z]
				(Both Saros: Antigonos 6)
437	Alexander IV 6	9 Nov 312 – 8 Nov 311	3 Apr 311 [aa] – no later than a day in 10–19 May 311 [bb]	Antigonos 7 [z]
			at the latest by a day in 11–20 May 311 [bb] – 21 Apr 310	(Solar Saros: Alexander IV 6)
				(Saros Canon: Seleukos 1)
				Alexander IV 6
				(Solar Saros: Alexander IV 6)
				(Saros Canon: Seleukos 1)
438	Alexander IV 7 [cc]	9 Nov 311 – 8 Nov 310	22 Apr 310 – 9 Apr 309	Alexander IV 7 [cc]
				(Solar Saros: Alexander IV 7)
				(Saros Canon: Seleukos 2)
439	Alexander IV 8 [cc]	9 Nov 310 – 7 Nov 309	10 Apr 309 [dd] – 29 Mar 308	Alexander IV 8 [cc]
				(Solar Saros: Alexander IV 8)
				(Saros Canon: Seleukos 3)
440	Alexander IV 9 [cc]	8 Nov 309 – 7 Nov 308	30 Mar 308 – 17 Apr 307	Alexander IV 9 [cc]
				(Solar Saros: Alexander IV 9)
				(Saros Canon: Seleukos 4)

UPDATES TO ACHAEMENID CHRONOLOGY

Era of Nabo-nassar	Egyptian Regnal Year	Length of 365-day Egyptian year (some Julian dates other than new year derived from lunar dates may be 1 or 2 days off)	Length of Year in Babylon (having been derived from lunar dates, these Julian dates may be 1 or 2 days off)	Babylonian Regnal Year
441	Alexander IV 10	8 Nov 308 – 7 Nov 307	**18 Apr 307 – 6 Apr 306**	Alexander IV 10
				(Solar Saros: Alexander IV 10)
				(Saros Canon: Seleukos 5)
442	Alexander IV 11	8 Nov 307 – 7 Nov 306	**7 Apr 306 – 25 Mar 305**	Alexander IV 11
				(Solar Saros: Alexander IV 11)
				(Saros Canon: Seleukos 6)
443	Alexander IV 12	8 Nov 306 – 6 Nov 305	**26 Mar 305 – 13 Apr 304**[ee]	Alexander IV 12? and/or Seleukos I 7?[ee]
				(Both Saros: Seleukos 7)
444	Alexander IV 13 Ptolemy I Soter 1	7 Nov 305 – at least until a day in 6 Jan–4 Feb 304[ff] no earlier than a day in 7 Jan–5 Feb[ff] – 6 Nov 304	**14 Apr 304 – 3 Apr 303**[gg]	Seleukos I 8[gg]
				(Both Saros: Seleukos 8)
(445	Ptolemy I Soter 2	7 Nov 304 – 6 Nov 303)	(**4 Apr 303 – 22 Apr 302**	Seleukos I 9)

68

Notes to the table

[a] Around this time, Artaxerxes III probably reconquered Egypt and Nectanebo II's reign ended. Nectanebo II was obviously not a ruler of the Achaemenid empire and has therefore been placed between parentheses.

[b] Owing to BM 48063 + 48069 (Sachs and Hunger 1988: 162–65), it is now certain that daylight of 12 Apr 339 B.C.E. equals daylight of Month 1 (Nisanu) Day 1 in Babylonian astronomical tablets and presumably also in all of the city of Babylon (already provisionally identified so in *PD* 35).

[c] This is the Babylonian Month 6 (Ululu) in 338 B.C.E. According to tablet BM 71537, Artaxerxes III died and his son Arses (Artaxerxes IV) succeeded him in that month (see §5).

[d] It is not clear how the days from the beginning of the reign to the beginning of Egyptian Year 1 on the first new year of the reign were designated in Egypt. The beginning of Egyptian Year 1 was itself predated from the postdated Babylonian new year in the following spring.

[e] In Ptolemy's Royal Canon, Arses' reign begins with his Year 1 on this day, which is a new year as are all the beginnings of the Canon's reigns. His predecessor Artaxerxes III's reign spans 21 full Egyptian years in the Canon.

[f] The component "September" of this date is derived from a report in Diodoros (XVII 5,4) that Arses had a third year and the component "18 Mar 335 B.C.E." is derived from an Aramaic papyrus from Wadi Daliyeh (see §6).

[g] In Ptolemy's Royal Canon, Darius III's reign begins with his Year 1 on this day, which is a new year as are the beginnings of all the Canon's reigns. His predecessor Arses' reign spans two full Egyptian years in the Canon.

[h] Alexander conquered Egypt in late 332 B.C.E., that is, November or December of that year, probably not as late as January 331 B.C.E. (see §7). It is not known whether he was already recognized as Pharaoh on the Egyptian new year of 14 Nov 332 B.C.E.

[i] It is not certain whether Darius 5 had an actual Egyptian Year 5. If Alexander conquered Egypt after new year of 14 Nov 332 B.C.E., he may have had.

[j] In Ptolemy's Royal Canon, Alexander III's reign begins with his Year 1 on this day, a new year just like all the beginnings of the Canon's reigns. His predecessor Darius III's reign spans four full Egyptian years in the Canon.

[k] 1 Oct 311 B.C.E. is the date of the battle of Gaugamela, that is, Month 6 (Ululu) Day 24, according to tablet BM 36761 (Hunger 1988: 178–79). On this day or more probably soon after, Babylonian began dating documents according to Alexander. Alexander entered Babylon within a couple of weeks after the battle.

[l] The accession year is attested in tablet Harvard Semitic Museum 1893.5.29 (Boiy 2002a: 28).

[m] The Solar Saros and the Saros Lunar Canon, two astronomical texts, both begin Alexander's reign with his Year 1 on this day. On this day, Alexander was in his actual Egyptian Year 2 and also began his actual Babylonian Year 7.

[n] Owing to BM 35024 + 35064 + 35087 + 35618 + 35632 + 45955 (Sachs and Hunger 1988: 192–95, 204), it is now certain that daylight of 7 Apr 325 B.C.E. equals daylight of Month 1 (Nisanu) Day 1 in Babylonian astronomical tablets and presumably in all of Babylon (already provisionally identified so in *PD* 36).

[o] In Ptolemy's Royal Canon, Philip Arridaios' reign begins with his Year 1 on this day, a new year as with the beginnings of all the Canon's reigns. His predecessor Alexander III's reign spans 8 full Egyptian years in the Canon.

[p] Alexander the Great died on this day (Depuydt 1997d). He was then in his actual Egyptian Year 9, attested in Demotic Papyrus Strassburg 1, and in his actual Babylonian Year 14.

[q] The Solar Saros and the Saros Lunar Canon, two astronomical texts, both begin Philip Arridaios' reign with his Year 1 on this day. In both Saros genres, Alexander's reign lasts seven full Babylonian calendars, counted as Years 1 through 7, until the day before the Babylonian new year of 14 Apr 323 B.C.E. Owing to BM 45766 (Sachs and Hunger 1988: 204–7), it is now certain that daylight of 14 Apr 323 B.C.E. (as opposed to the 15 April obtained by computation in *PD* 36) equals daylight of Month 1 (Nisanu) Day 1 in Babylonian astronomical tablets and presumably in all of Babylon.

[r] Owing to Rm 792 + BM 32240 + 32430 + 32489 (Sachs and Hunger 1988: 209–19) and BM 34093 + 35758 (Sachs and Hunger 1988: 220–29), it is now certain that daylight of 4 Apr 322 B.C.E. equals daylight of Month 1 (Nisanu)

Day 1 in Babylonian astronomical tablets and presumably in all of Babylon (already provisionally identified so in *PD* 36).

s The latest known dated Egyptian source belonging to Arridaios' reign is dated to Month 3 of his Year 8, that is, 9 Jan–7 Feb 317 B.C.E., namely Demotic Papyrus Bibliothèque nationale 219 (§9.1). According to tablet BM 32238, Arridaios' reign ended on 26 Dec 317 B.C.E. Egyptian documents were dated to Arridaios beyond this date, but no later than 9 Apr 316 B.C.E. because 10 Apr 316 B.C.E. is the date of the earliest dated Egyptian dosumented dated to the reign of Alexander IV.

t The reign of Antigonos begins here in the Saros Canon with his Year 1 (see §§9.2.3.3–4). It is the beginning of Year 7 of Arridaios in the Saros Canon.

u On 26 Dec 317 B.C.E., Philip Arridaios' reign ended according to tablet BM 32238. Presumably, he died on this day or shortly before (see §9.1). But cuneiform tablets kept being dated to Arridaios for some months after his death, until at least Month 7 Day 19 of Year 8, that is, *ca.* 9 Oct 316 B.C.E. (§9.2.3.2). The latter part of his Babylonian Year 7 and all dates in his Babylonian Year 8 are therefore posthumous.

v 10 Apr 316 B.C.E. is the date of the earliest known dated Egyptian source of Alexander IV's reign, namely Demotic Papyrus Loeb 27 (see §9.2.2). But presumably, dating Alexander IV's began earlier, since Philip's date of death is 26 Dec 317 B.C.E.

w The latest dated tablet of Arridaios' reign, BM 79012, is dated to *ca.* 9 Oct 316 B.C.E. (see §9.2.3.2).

x The reign of Antigonos begins here in the Saros Canon with his Year 3 (see §§9.2.3.3–4).

y Documents are dated to Alexander IV at least until Month 4 Day 8 of his Year 2, or *ca.* 21 Jul 315 B.C.E., the date of Idumean ostrakon no. 27 in Porten's and Yardeni's list of "45(+3) Documents according to Macedonian Rulers" (Porten and Yardeni 2008 [see table at the end]), also temporary no. 1254 in the list of the Institute for the Study of Aramaic Papyri (ISAP). The latest known dated cuneiform tablet is dated to Month 3 (Simanu) of his Year 2, or *ca.* 15 Jun–14 Jul 315 B.C.E., the date of *CT* 49 13 (Jursa 1997: 132–33; cf. Boiy 1998, 2000: 119, and 2006: 71). The earliest date for Antigonos is Month 4 Day 7 of his Year 3, or *ca.* 20 July 315 B.C.E., which is the date of Idumean ostrakon no. 26 in Porten's and Yardeni's afore-mentioned list, ISAP's temporary no. 1546. The transition from Alexander IV to Antigonos can therefore safely and fairly sharply be dated to around 20–21 Jul 315 B.C.E. The fact that the earliest date for Antigonos is a day earlier than the latest date for Alexander IV in dates from Idumean ostraka is no cause for concern. Around the transition from one reign to another, uncertainty regarding the identity of the ruler to whom a document should be dated is not altogether unexpected. It does mean that the reign of Alexander IV ended before 20 Jul 315 B.C.E. The earliest dated cuneiform tablet of Antigonos' reign, *CT* 49 34, is dated to Month 9 of his Year 3, that is, *ca.* 12 Dec 315 B.C.E.–*ca.* 6 Jan 314 B.C.E. (see §9.2.3.2). In sum, the emergence of the Idumean ostraka in recent years has added much precision in dating to the transition from Alexander IV to Antigonos.

z Perhaps tablets were sometimes dated jointly to Antigonos and Alexander IV, the latter's regnal year being one lower than the former's, as presumably in tablet *AION Suppl.* 77 87 (see §9.2.3.3).

aa The beginning of the Seleucid era was in effect backdated to this day when Seleukos died and it was decided to continue to count years in perpetuity according to his reign. The king list from Uruk also begins with Year 1 of Seleukos on this day (§9.2.3.5).

bb The earliest dated tablet of Alexander IV's reign, BM 22022, is dated to *ca.* 11–20 May 311 B.C.E. (see §9.2.3.5). Presumably Seleukos had conquered Babylon by this time and had begun dating by Alexander IV, as he had when in charge of Babylon in 316–315 B.C.E. (see earlier in the table).

cc Some time in these years or very close to it, Alexander IV was put to death and the dating by his reign became fictional for a few years.

dd Owing to BM 40078 + 40105 (Sachs and Hunger 1988: 232–39), it is now certain that daylight of 10 Apr 309 B.C.E. equals daylight of Month 1 (Nisanu) Day 1 in Babylonian astronomical tablets and presumably in all of Babylon (already provisionally identified so in *PD* 37).

ee Due to a lack of sources, it is not certain how this year was dated in business documents and colophons of literary manuscripts, whether partly to both kings or entirely to one of the two kings, but probably at least partly to Seleukos. Both the Solar Saros and the Saros Lunar Canon assign the entire year to Seleukos and so do the king lists from Babylon and Uruk (§9.2.3.5). The six preceding full Babylonian years from spring 311 B.C.E. to spring 305 B.C.E. are styled as Years 1–6 of Alexander IV in the list from Babylon and as Years 1–6 of Seleukos in the list from Uruk.

ff The latest dated Egyptian documents of Alexander IV's reign, namely Demotic Papyri Louvre 2427 and 2440, are dated to 6 Jan–4 Feb 304 B.C.E. (see §9.2.2.).

gg This year in all probability was dated in its entirety to the reign of Seleukos (I). But strictly speaking, the date of the earliest known dated cuneiform document of the reign of Seleukos, namely BM 78603, is *ca.* 16 Apr 304 B.C.E. (see §9.2.3.5).

APPENDIX I:
ERRATA IN PREVIOUS PUBLICATIONS

[References are to page, column [a = left; b = right], and *line*.]

Depuydt 1995a
   (The Date of Death of Artaxerxes I. *Welt des Orients* 26: 86–96.)

(92,*4*) For "the earliest XII/14" read "the earliest attested double date XII/14." (92,*23*) For "425" read "424."

Depuydt 1995b
   (Regnal Years and Civil Calendar in Achaemenid Egypt. *Journal of Egyptian Archaeology* 81: 151–73.)

(152,note 5) As regards general studies of Achaemenid Egypt, add Bresciani 1958. (157,*19*) For "the dates span the period 6 March–19 December 475" read "the preserved dates and those restored by the editors (Bezalel Porten and Ada Yardeni) span the period from 6 March (Month 3 Day 17) to 14 December (Month 12 Day 30) 475 (B.C.E.)." (157,*14–21*) The Aramaic Customs Account (document "C3.7" in vol. 3 of Porten and Yardeni 1986–99) is dated to Xerxes I, but Briant and Descat (1998: 60–62) and Porten (1990: 17) have proposed Artaxerxes I as an alternative. (157, note 22,*1*) For "Month 6 Day 22" read "Month 8 Day 22." (158,*19*) For "evidence from" read "evidence for." (158,*31*) For "586" read "486." (158,*33*) For "25 December" read "25 December 424." (159, note 27,*7*) For "2 January 465," read "2 January 464." (169,*20*) For "*2 Jan 525–1 Jan 524*" (that is, Year 5 of Cambyses) read "*2 Jan 525–31 Dec 525.*" (171, note j) For "4–8 August 565" read "4–8 August 465." (171,*37–48*) For "I *3ḫt* 1," "II *3ḫt* 1," and so on, read "I *3ḫt*," "II *3ḫt*," and so on. (173,*16*) For "(Vienna, 1988)" read "(Vienna, 1889)."

Depuydt 1995d
   ("More Valuable than All Gold": Ptolemy's Royal Canon and Babylonian Chronology. *Journal of Cuneiform Studies* 47: 97–117.)

(97,a,*12*) For "vol. 3" read "vol. 1." (100,b,*32*) For "its covers" read "it covers." (101,b,*9–12*) As regards the "eclipse reports dating to the second half of the eighth century BCE," see now Walker (1997: 17–18), also citing publications by Abraham Sachs and Peter Huber. (107,a,*37*) For "Month 4 Day 16" read "Month 4 Day 14." (110,b,*3*) For "Cambyses 3" read "Cambyses 4." (110,b,*5*) For "*2 Jan 525–31 Dec 524*" (that is, Year 5 of Cambyses) read "*2 Jan 525–31 Dec 525.*" (110,b) Note that two 365-day Egyptian years (Years 222 and 223 from Nabonassar) end in 525 B.C.E. (which is a leap year of 366 days), namely on 1 January 525 B.C.E. and again after 365 days on 31 December 525 B.C.E., and also that two 365-day Egyptian years (Years 227 and 228 from Nabonassar) begin in 521 B.C.E. (which is a leap year of 366 days), namely on 1 January 521 B.C.E. and again after 365 days on 31 December 521 B.C.E. (cf. Depuydt 1995c: 194, note 8). (115b,*36*) For "Hinrich" read "Hinrichs."

THREE ADDENDA.

(1) First addendum concerning the statement at 115,b,*19–22*:

   [I]t remains unknown whether Nabonassar already ruled on 26 February 747 B.C.E., at the beginning of the Era named after him.

It now appears that he did. In fact, not only his accession year but also his Year 1 had begun before 26 Feb 747 B.C.E. Year 1 begins four days earlier on 22 Feb 747 B.C.E.! In this respect at least, Oppert (1897: 159) was right and Kugler (1907–24, vol. 2.2.2: 357) was wrong. The cuneiform eclipse tablet BM 41985 (Hunger 2001: 2–3 [no. 1]) dates an eclipse possibility to Month 12 of an accession year. The accession year must be Nabonassar's and the eclipse possibility must be that of 6 Feb 747 B.C.E. There was no month 13. Nabonassar's Year 1 therefore began half a lunar month later. The eclipse of Year 2 Month 5 is described as total. Its totality could not be seen in Babylon itself (Steele in Hunger 2001: 3), but could be in the lands east of Babylon.

(2) Second addendum concerning the statement at 99,b,*17–19*:

The Canon shifts from Babylon to Alexandria with Numbers 31, 32, and 33 [that is, Alexander III, Arridaios, and Alexander IV].

In fact, the shift occurs in the transition from Darius III to Alexander III, that is between Number 30 and Number 31 (see §7 above).

(3) Third addendum concerning the statement at 113,b,*end*:

[T]he postdating system was abandoned from Alexander onwards.

This statement only applies to the partly artificial years of the Canon. In actuality, the first king whose reign was not postdated was Philip Arridaios (see §7 above).

Depuydt 1996
    ("(Egyptian Regnal Dating" under Cambyses and the Date of the Persian Conquest. In *Studies in Honor of William Kelly Simpson*, edited by Peter Der Manuelian. Pp. 179–90. Boston: Museum of Fine Arts, Department of Ancient Egyptian, Nubian, and "Near Eastern Art.")

(190,*13*) For "*2 Jan 525–1 Jan 524*" (that is, Year 5 of Cambyses) read "*2 Jan 525–31 Dec 525.*"

Depuydt 1997
    (The Time of Death of Alexander the Great: 11 June 323 B.C. (–322), ca.4:00–5:00 PM. *Die Welt des Orients* 28: 117–35.)

(126,*16*) For "about 16 hours" read "about 14 hours." (127,*18*) For "last crescent visibility" read "last crescent invisibility." (129,*28*) For "comprises of" read "comprises." (133, note 35,*4*) For "(19941" read "(1994)." (135,*3,7*) For "Julian-Gregorian day" read "julian day (j.d.)." (135,*1*) For "11 June 323 B.C. is [j.d.] 1 603 610" read "... is j.d. 1 603 609.00–1 603 610.00" (similar corrections need to be applied to the other dates at p. 135), because j.d. numbers are strictly speaking cardinal, even if that still makes 11 Jun 323 B.C.E. the 1,603,609th day of the Julian day count and even if I indicated that I understood "1 603 610" as an ordinal number by adding specifically "all of January 4713 B.C. being the first day or day 1." For daylight of 11 Jun 323 B.C.E as the date transmitted in the cuneiform record, see— independently—Walker 1997: 25.

Depuydt 2002
    (The Date of Death of Jesus of Nazareth. *Journal of the American Oriental Society* 122: 466–80.)

(467,b,*21*) For "Rufius," read "Fufius" ("Rufius" and "Fufius" both occur in the sources, but *Paulys Real-Encyclopädie* prefers "Fufius"). (474,a,*19*) For "מ" (non-final form of Hebrew letter *mim*) read "ם" (final form). (475,*12*) Move "2:41 p.m." up one line. (475,*14*) For "Year 5" read "Year 15." (475,*32,34*) Add "Year 8" under "12 Thoth" in date no. 11 and "Year 13" under 9 Hathor in date no. 12, both dates having *two* year dates. (475,*26*) For "Artaxerxes" read "Artaxerxes I." (479,a,*9*) For "*Egypt*" read "*Egypte*."

Depuydt 2006a
    (Saite and Persian Egypt, 664–332 BC [Dynasties 26–31, Psammetichus I to Alexander's Conquest of Egypt]. In Hornung et al. 2006: 265–83.)

(265,*5*) For "can dated" read "can be dated." (265,*11*) Move note 1 from after "... detail." to after "... time." in line 6. Addendum: for the Ḥašbâ tablet (*BE* IX no. 109), see also Kugler 1907–24, vol. 2.2.2: 389.

Depuydt 2006b
    (Foundations of Day-exact Chronology. In Hornung et al. 2006: 458–470.)

(466,*15*) For "five days less" read "five days more." (467,note 13,*2*) For "Johnson" read "Jonsson" (as added correctly to the last proofs). (470,*10*) For "Year 5" read "Year 15." (470,*28,30*) Add "Year 8" under "12 Thoth" in date no. 11 and "Year 13" under 9 Hathor in date no. 12, both dates having *two* year dates (as reported to me by C.O. Jonsson and correctly noted in Depuydt 1995b: 162).

APPENDIX II:
REMARKS ON MOST RECENT PUBLICATIONS
(BOIY 2006, PORTEN AND YARDENI 2008)

1. Chronology of the Years from the Death of Alexander (323 B.C.E.) till about 300 B.C.E. in light of Boiy 2006 and Porten and Yardeni 2008

The present investigation was completed in the fall of 2007. After it was submitted to the publisher in the spring of 2008, Bezalel Porten drew my attention to the following two recent studies and kindly sent me an offprint of his own, the latter. This offprint includes a sheet with errata printed at the end after page 249. I assume it is not included in the book, which I have not seen.

> Tom Boiy. Aspects chronologiques de la période de transition (350–300). In: *La transition entre l'empire achéménide et les royaumes hellénistiques*, edited by Pierre Briant and Francis Joannès. Persika, 9. Pp. 37–100. Paris: De Boccard, 2006.

> Bezalel Porten and Ada Yardeni. The Chronology of the Idumean Ostraca in the Decade or so after the Death of Alexander the Great and Its Relevance for Historical Events. In: *Treasures on Camels' Humps: Historical and Literary Studies from the Ancient Near East Presented to Israel Eph'al*, edited by Mordechai Cogan and Dan'el Kahn. Pp. 237–49. Jerusalem: The Hebrew University Magnes Press, 2008.

The first study was probably just being catalogued in academic libraries around the time when this investigation was being written. From it, I also learned about the following recent article, which I have not seen:

> G.R.F. Assar, Parthian Calendars at Babylon and Seleucia on the Tigris. *Iran* 41 (2003): 171–91.

A couple of items of information derived from these two studies have been incorporated in the main text, as have bibliographical items into the bibliography. What could not be incorporated is described below.

Boiy's study shows how much our understanding of all facets—Macedonian, Babylonian, Egyptian, Aramaic—of the chronological structure of the three decades following Alexander's first conquests (*ca.* 333 B.C.E.–*ca.* 304 B.C.E.) have emerged with some degree of clarity in just the last decade, after having been opaque for centuries, especially with regard to Mesopotamia. The historical events of those three decades have long been known in some detail, even before the decipherment of hieroglyphic and cuneiform writing in the nineteenth century. Classical sources describing them, foremost Diodoros, have been accessible since the Renaissance. It is mainly owed to Babylonian and Aramaic sources that it became possible to put the chronology of the period in order. Two sets of sources have been the most valuable in this respect. They are Babylonian astronomical texts, especially the Diaries, and Aramaic ostraka from Idumea, an arid country south of Judaea centered around the Dead Sea that was converted to Judaism in the late second century B.C.E. The two sets have become generally accessible only fairly recently. Babylonian cuneiform tablets of astronomical purport have made their way to museums in the west already from the late nineteenth century. But it is only in the last 20 years or so that their contents have become accessible in a manner that could more directly benefit the study of chronology and history. To be singled out is Sachs's and Hunger's edition of the Babylonian Diaries. About the second set, Porten and Yardeni (2008: 237) write that "[i]n the last decade or so there have turned up on the antiquities market more than 1700 legible Aramaic ostraca from Idumea."

The chronology of the period lasting from the death of Alexander III on 11 Jun 323 B.C.E. until about 300 B.C.E. may be summarized as follows. Seven episodes may be distinguished in the way documents are dated in Babylon and presumably most elsewhere in ancient West Asia. By contrast, only four episodes need to be distinguished in Egypt.

UPDATES TO ACHAEMENID CHRONOLOGY

DATING IN BABYLON AND PRESUMABLY ALL OF ANCIENT WEST ASIA

1. by the living king Philip (until his death on 26 Dec 317 B.C.E.)
2. by the deceased king Philip (until at least *ca.* 19 Dec 316 B.C.E.)
3. by the living king Alexander IV, with Seleukos (later king Seleukos I) as caretaker (from *ca.* 20 Dec 316 B.C.E. at the earliest until *ca.* 20/21 Jul 315 B.C.E.)
4. mainly by Antigonos, but not styled as king (apparently also occasionally, or additionally, by Alexander IV) (from *ca.* 20/21 Jul 315 B.C.E. until *ca.* 10–19 May 311 B.C.E. at the latest)
5. again by the living king Alexander IV, with Seleukos (later king Seleukos I) as caretaker (from 11–20 May 311 B.C.E. at the latest till the death of Alexander IV sometime in 311–309 B.C.E.)
6. by the deceased king Alexander IV, with Seleukos effectively in charge (from the death of Alexander IV sometime in 311–309 B.C.E. until *ca.* 15 Apr 304 B.C.E. at the latest)
7. by king Seleukos I (from *ca.* 16 Apr 304 B.C.E. at the latest)

DATING IN EGYPT

1. by the living king Philip (until at least 9 Jan–7 Feb 316 B.C.E. [Philip had died shortly before on 26 Dec 317 B.C.E., but later dates presumably involve the assumption that he was still alive])
2. by the living king Alexander IV, with Ptolemy (later king Ptolemy I) as caretaker (from 10 Jan–8 Feb 316 B.C.E. at the earliest until the death of Alexander IV sometime in 311–309 B.C.E.)
3. by the deceased king Alexander IV, with Ptolemy effectively in charge (from the death of Alexander IV sometime in 311–309 B.C.E. until at least Month 3 Year 13, or 6 Jan–4 Feb 304 B.C.E.)
4. by king Ptolemy I (from 7 Jan–5 Feb 304 B.C.E. at the earliest)

The episodes in Egypt are three fewer than those in Babylon for the following three reasons: (1) there was no dating by the deceased king Philip; (2) there was no dating by Antigonos, who never ruled in Egypt; (3) owing to the absence of Antigonos, the episode in which documents are dated by the living king Alexander IV is not split into two.

Evidence supporting the lists above is as follows. A more comprehensive listing of the evidence remains desirable.

DATING IN BABYLON AND PRESUMABLY ALL OF ANCIENT WEST ASIA: EVIDENCE

1. living king Philip
    date of death of Philip in cuneiform tablet BM 32238: Month 9 Day 27 [Year 7], or 25/26 Dec 317 B.C.E. (evening to evening) (see §9.1)
2. deceased king Philip
    date of latest cuneiform tablet, BM 79012: Month 7 Day 18 Year 8, or *ca.* 9 Oct 316 B.C.E. (see §9.2.3.2; Jursa 1997: 133)
    date of latest Idumean ostrakon: Month 9 Day 30 Year 8, or *ca.* 19 Dec 316 B.C.E., although Philip is not named (Porten and Yardeni 2008: 249 no. 21)
3. living king Alexander IV, with Seleukos as caretaker
    date of earliest cuneiform tablet: Year 1 is attested in BM 78948, apparently without month and day date (at least none is given in Jursa 1997: 133)
    date of earliest Idumean ostrakon: Month 3 Day 6 Year 2, or *ca.* 20 Jun 315 B.C.E. (Porten and Yardeni 2008: 249 no. 22)
    date of latest cuneiform tablet, *CT* 49 13: Month 3 Year 2, or *ca.* 15 Jun–14 Jul 315 B.C.E. (Jursa 1997: 132–33)
    date of latest Idumean ostrakon: Month 4 Day 8 Year 2, or *ca.* 21 Jul 315 B.C.E. (Porten and Yardeni 2008: 249 no. 27)
4. Antigonos, apparently occasionally alongside king Alexander IV
    date of earliest Idumean ostrakon: Month 4 Day 7 Year 3, or *ca.* 20 Jul 315 B.C.E. (Porten and Yardeni 2008: 249 no. 26)
    date of earliest cuneiform tablet: Month 9 Year 3, or *ca.* 12 Dec 315 B.C.E.–*ca.* 6 Jan 314 B.C.E. (Boiy 2000: 119)
    dates of Idumean ostraka dated to Alexander IV: Month 1 Day 6 Year 3, or *ca.* 10 Apr 314 B.C.E.; Month 3 Day 25 Year 5, or *ca.* 5 Jul 312 B.C.E.; Month 11 Day 22 Year 5, or *ca.* 22 Feb 311 B.C.E. (twice) (Porten and Yardeni 2008: 249 nos. 36, 40, 43, and 44)
5. again living king Alexander IV, with Seleukos (later king Seleukos I) as caretaker

date of earliest cuneiform tablet, BM 22022: Month 2 Day 10-19 Year 6, or *ca.* 11-20 May 311 B.C.E. (Boiy 2000: 119 note 19)
6. deceased king Alexander IV, with Seleukos effectively in charge
   cuneiform tablets dated to Year 11 of Alexander: *CT* 49 25 and *ZA* 3 148-49 (Boiy 2006: 49)
7. king Seleukos I
   date of earliest cuneiform tablet, BM 78603 or *CT* 4 plate 29*d*: Month 1 Day 3 Year 8, or 16 Apr 304 B.C.E. (McEwan 1985; Boiy 2000: 120 with note 25)

DATING IN EGYPT: EVIDENCE

1. living king Philip
   date of latest papyrus, Demotic Papyrus Bibliothèque nationale 219: Month 3 Year 8, or 9 Jan-7 Feb 316 B.C.E.
2. living king Alexander IV, with Ptolemy (later king Ptolemy I) as caretaker
   date of earliest papyrus, Demotic Papyrus Loeb 27: Month 6 Day 2 Year 1, or 10 Apr 316 B.C.E. (Skeat 1969: 27)
3. deceased king Alexander IV, with Ptolemy effectively in charge
   date of latest papyri, Louvre 2427 and 2440 (in Demotic): Month 3 Year 13, or 6 Jan-4 Feb 304 B.C.E. (Skeat 1969: 28)
4. king Ptolemy I
   there are no papyri from Year 1 (Pestman 1967: 13)

Boiy's study (2006) is in part a survey of earlier work, including his own (Boiy 1998, 2000, 2001, 2002a, and 2002b). Porten's and Yardeni's article surveys all the chronological information that has been extracted from the Idumean ostraka. There is a total of 31 texts dated by Macedonian rulers and Porten and Yardeni believe they can expand the number on the basis of paleography and prosopography. Boiy's article also includes information derived from Idumean ostraka, in part obtained through personal communications by Porten.

2. Notes to Boiy 2006

2.1. Results

First, it is shown that Arses took the name Artaxerxes (IV) and, second, that he had an accession year (MU.SAG) as had been generally assumed (pp. 45-47).

Third, among the useful tables contained in the article is one listing tablets with their year dates year by year for the period from Year 9 of Artaxerxes III to Year 12 of the Seleucid Era (pp. 47-51). In this connection, one might also refer to the convenient table reflecting the chronology of the contemporary cuneiform documents in an article by Joannès in the same volume (Joannès 2006: 103). Another table lists the lengths of all the lunar months in days, either 29 or 30, in the period from 350 B.C.E. to 300 B.C.E., updating Parker's and Dubberstein's list (1956) where necessary (pp. 89-95). One wished a similar update existed for the entire span of years covered by Parker and Dubberstein, 626 B.C.E.-75 C.E., and in fact for the entire period in which Babylonian astronomers must have fixed the length of every lunar month, presumably from 747 B.C.E. onward.

Fourth, as a general rule, Years 1-6 of Alexander the Great do not exist in cuneiform documents because Alexander began the Babylonian count of regnal years with Year 7 at new year in the spring of 330 B.C.E., following the defeat of Darius III at Gaugamela on 1 Oct 331 B.C.E. The interval from 1 Oct 331 B.C.E. to new year in the spring of 330 B.C.E. was his accession year. Tablet *BRM* 2 51 would evidence a different manner of counting if the name of the ruler to whose Year 6 the tablet is dated is to be read as Alexander (the Great); the matter remains doubtful, however (pp. 51-52).

Fifth, a sizeable portion of the study (pp. 64-86) is devoted to the dating of the macropolitical history of Mesopotomia in the decade lasting from 321 B.C.E. to 311 B.C.E. Constant reference is made to alternative proposals by others, especially in more recent times by Brian Bosworth and Pat Wheatley. The debate has long centered around a choice between a high chronology and a low chronology. Boiy defends a mixture of the two (see now also Boiy 2007, which reached me too late for a report in the present study). I have not studied the matter in detail. Nevertheless, it seems clear that Boiy's analysis has been the first to benefit from the straightening of the period's chronology in light of the Babylonian and Aramaic evidence. It seems to me that this benefit would lend his views a distinct advantage.

Sixth, the relevance of the Idumean ostraka is highlighted in anticipation of the fuller discussion by Porten and Yardeni (2008).

2.2. Observations

(1) As regards terminology, writing in French, Boiy uses the term *antidater*, apparently as an equivalent of English "antedate." Latin *ante* "before" indeed appears in French as *anti*, as in *anticiper* "anticipate." The problem with *antidater* is that, in French, *anti* is much more often an equivalent of Greek ἀντί "against, opposite," as in *anticorps* "antibody" and *antigel* "antifreeze." *Prédater* might therefore be a more suitable choice, with *pré–* deriving from Latin *prae*. Accordingly, *prédater* would conveniently serve as the Latinate counterpart of the author's own *postdater*, featuring Latin *post* "after." Greek for "before" is otherwise πρό, with Greek ἀντί "against" corresponding to Latin *contra*. However, *prodater* would rather call to mind Latin *pro* "instead of" rather than Greek πρό "before." In addition, *prodater* would suffer the disadvantage of being a Greek-Latin hybrid.

(2) Concerning year-dating in Egypt, Boiy (2006: 38) writes, "Dans la tradition égyptienne d'antidatation… le début du nouveau règne est le nouvel an qui précède l'accession au trône." This statement implies that a Pharaoh's reign began before he ascended to the throne, which is impossible. Regnal Year 1 began on the day of accession and regnal Year 2 on the first new year. Antedating or predating is therefore better defined as follows: a regnal year of a certain number begins on the new year *preceding* the anniversary of the accession marking the beginning of the full 365-day period with the same number as the regnal year. For example, the beginning of regnal Year 2 *precedes* the anniversary that marks the beginning of the second full 365-day period. It is only in Ptolemy's Canon and in similar chronological tools that the practice described by Boiy was applied, namely artificially backdating the beginning of the reign to the preceding New Year's Day. In this connection, at p. 40, line 3, for "Xerxes III" read "Xerxes I."

(3) Arridaios died in his Year 7 on 26 Dec 317 B.C.E., but contemporary documents kept being dated by his reign into the calendar year that overlapped with his Year 8. The rest of that same Babylonian calendar year, from late 316 B.C.E. to the Babylonian new year in spring 315 B.C.E., was apparently Alexander IV's Year 1. The period from new year in spring 315 B.C.E. to summer 315 B.C.E. was Alexander IV's Year 2. The Solar Saros assigns the interval from late 316 B.C.E. to the Babylonian new year in spring 315 B.C.E. to Year 8 of Arridaios. Boiy (2006: 44) describes this procedure as postdating. "Postdating" may not be the proper term. What happened is as follows.

First of all, the Solar Saros clearly antedates or predates the reigns of Arridaios and Antigonos. Arridaios' reign begins with the Babylonian new year *preceding* his accession to the throne; Antigonos' reign begins with the Babylonian new year *preceding* his accession to the throne in what he styled as his Year 3. Antedating is the natural choice if regnal Year 1 begins with the accession. If postdating were applied, the numbers of the regnal years would differ by one from the numbers of the actual regnal years. As a result of antedating, Alexander IV's Year 2 was obliterated and assigned to Antigonos. That left only Alexander IV's Year 1, half a year or less. There were two options. The first was antedating Alexander IV's reign by assigning the entire Babylonian calendar year from spring 316 B.C.E. to spring 315 B.C.E. to him. The result would be a reign of just one year. Postdating Arridaios' Year 8 was not an option because, by the definition of postdating, Year 8 would then begin with the Babylonian new year in spring 315 B.C.E. But it already began in spring 316 B.C.E. and could hardly have two beginnings. The second option that was in fact applied is therefore better described as *extending* Arridaios' reign for some months to include Alexander IV's Year 1.

(4) In tablet BM 32238 (Hunger 2001: 6–7 [no. 2]), one reads as follows:
   Rev.´ V´
      12´ Month 9, Day 27, Pill[i-....] (Philip Arridaios)
      13´ Year 2 of Antigonos

According to Boiy (p. 52), there is a "problem" in the form of a "contradiction" in that he expects "Year 1 of Antigonos" instead of "Year 2 of Antigonos." He adduces an explanation by Assar (2003: 185) while pointing to its problems. But in fact, there is neither problem nor contradiction. "Year 2" is fully expected. Boiy and Assar assume that lines 12´ and 13´ refer to the same Babylonian calendar year. There is no doubt that Arridaios died in the Babylonian year lasting from spring 317 B.C.E. to spring 316 B.C.E. By every attested count, this is the same year as Antigonos' virtual Year 1 and not his virtual Year 2. Antigonos reigned in actuality only from his Year 3 onward, beginning this year-count with the death of Arridaios. But astronomical texts in part backdate the beginning of Antigonos' reign to his virtual Year 1, which begins in the spring of 317 B.C.E., even before the death of Arridaios.

"Year 2" is fully expected because lines 12´ and 13´ do not refer to the same Babylonian calendar year. The tablet in question lists eclipse possibilities, which occur at five month or six month intervals (for the pattern of alternation of five and six, see Steele in Hunger, Sachs, and Steele 2001: 391). The death of Arridaios is clearly associated with the eclipse possibility that occurred on Month 9 Day 15, 12 days earlier. The next date must therefore pertain to the next eclipse possibility, in this case the one that fell six months later in Month 3 of the next calendar year. It is true that contemporary documents kept being dated in Babylon to Arridaios for several months after his death. But the author of the text in BM 32238 probably had no knowledge of how contemporary business documents were dated in the months following the death of Arridaios or at least did not take it into account. Clearly, what happened is that the reign of Antigonos was fictionally started earlier so that his Year 2 began in spring 316 B.C.E. In fact, this very eclipse possibility of Month 3 is explicitly dated to Antigonos' Year 2 in the Saros Canon (Aaboe, Britton, Henderson, Neugebauer, and Sachs 1991: 15). The Saros Canon dates the two previous eclipse possibilities, which preceded the death of Arridaios and fell six and twelve months earlier in Months 3 and 9 of the previous calendar year, to Year 1 of Antigonos. It is possible that they are also dated to Antigonos' Year 1 in BM 32238; the pertinent text has not survived. That would mean that, somewhat awkwardly, the death of Arridaios is dated to Year 1 of Antigonos. At all events, "Year 2 of Antigonos" is fully expected in BM 32238. There is no contradiction.

(5) Nor is there, as Boiy (2006: 90) assumes, any contradiction to be found in the following text in BM 34093 + 35758 (Sachs and Hunger 1988: 226–29), an excerpt of the Dairies pertaining to 322 B.C.E.:

   ´Rev
      (entry for Month 6)
      23´   The 27th, moonrise to sunrise: 17°. The 28th,. . . . The 30th equinox; I did not watch . . .
      . . .
      26´   Month 7, (the 1st of which was identical with) the 30th . . .

The text in line 26´ leaves no doubt that Month 6 had 29 days. This is expressed, as is the rule, by equating Day 1 of the following month with Day 30 of the previous month. However, in line 23´, there is reference to Day 30 of Month 6. Boiy assumes that this is an indication that Month 6 had 30 days, in seeming contradiction with what is stated in line 26´. An error of one day in the Diaries would falsify all astronomical computations. It was imperative that the lengths of all the lunar months over a period of eight centuries was fixed at 29 or 30. Babylonian astronomers derived the length of a month from the opening formula of the entry pertaining to the next month. If the entry began with "Day 1," then the previous month had 30 days. If the entry began with "Day 30" as a designation of Day 1 of the next month, then the previous month had 29 days. In the present case, therefore, Month 6 had 29 days. Still, the fact remains that the day that follows Day 29, the last of the month, was explicitly referred to as Day 30. It so happened in the year in question that the fall equinox fell on the first day of a month that was called Day 30 because the previous month had 29 days. That left no other choice but to refer to the day of the event as Day 30, whether at the end of the entry for Month 6 as is the case or in the beginning of the entry for Month 7. The opening formula of the entry for Month 7 otherwise left no doubt that Month 6 had had 29 days. In other words, when the day that follows Day 29 of a month that is 29 Days long is mentioned at the end of the entry for that 29-day month, it can only be referred to as Day 30, the same designation it receives if it is mentioned at the beginning of the entry for the next month.

ABBREVIATIONS AND REFERENCES

Aaboe, Asgar; and John P. Britton; J.A. Henderson; Otto Neugebauer; Abraham J. Sachs. 1991. Saros Cycle Dates and Related Babylonian Astronomical Texts. *Transactions of the American Philosophical Society*, New Series 81/6: 1–75.

AUWE = von Weiher 1998.

BE VIII.1 = Clay 1908.

BE X = Clay 1904.

Assar, G.R.F. 2003. Parthian Calendars at Babylon and Seleucia on the Tigris. *Iran* 41: 171–91. I have not seen this.

Beloch, Karl Julius. 1923. *Griechische Geschichte*, III: *Bis auf Aristoteles und die Eroberung Asiens*. Part 2. Berlin und Leipzig: Vereinigung wissenschaflticher Verleger and Walter de Gruyter & Co.

Bertin = 2889 unpublished tablet (cf. Bertin 1883).

Bertin, George. 1883. *Corpus of Babylonian Terra-Cotta Tablets, Principally Contracts*. vols. 1–6. London. Unpublished.

Bilfinger, Gustav. 1888. *Der bürgerliche Tag: Untersuchungen über den Beginn des Kalendertages im Classischen Altertum und im Christlichen Mittelalter*. Stuttgart: W. Kohlhammer.

BM 33342 = British Museum tablet published by Stolper (1983: 231–36).

BM 54557 = British Museum tablet published by Zawadzki (1995–96).

Boiy, Tom. 1998. Dating in Early Hellenistic Babylonia: Evidence on the Basis of CT 49 13, 1982.A.1853 and HSM 1893.5.6. *Nouvelles assyriologiques brèves et utilitaires (NABU)* 1998/134.

_____. 2000. Dating Methods during the Early Hellenistic Period. *Journal of Cuneiform Studies* 52: 115–21.

_____. 2001. Dating Problems in Cuneiform Tablets Concerning the Reign of Antigonus Monophthalmus. *Journal of the American Oriental Society* 121: 645–49.

_____. 2002a. The "Accession Year" in the Late Achaemenid and Early Hellenistic Period. In *Mining the Archives: Festschrift for Christopher Walker on the Occasion of His 60th Birthday, 4 October 2002*, edited by Cornelia Wunsch. Babylonische Archive, 1. Dresden: ISLET.

_____. 2002b. Early Hellenistic Chronography in Cuneiform Tradition. *Zeitschrift für Papyrologie und Epigraphik* 138: 249–55.

_____. 2006. Aspects chronologiques de la période de transition (350–300). In: *La transition entre l'empire achéménide et les royaumes hellénistiques*, edited by Pierre Briant and Francis Joannès. Persika, 9. Pp. 37–100. Paris: De Boccard.

_____. 2007. *Between High and Low: A Chronology of the Early Hellenic Period*. Oikumene Studien zur antiken Weltgeschichte, 5. Frankfurt am Main.

Brack-Bernsen, Lis. 1997. *Zur Entstehung der babylonischen Mondtheorie: Beobachtung und theoretische Berechnung von Mondphasen*. Boethius, 40. Stuttgart: Franz Steiner Verlag.

Bresciani, Edda. 1958. La Satrapia d'Egitto. *Studi Classici e Orientali* 7: 132–88.

Briant, Pierre. 1997. Bulletin d'histoire achéménide I. Topoi Orient-Occident, Supplément 1: 5–127.

____. 2001. *Bulletin d'histoire achéménide II, 1997–2000*. Paris: Thotm-éditions.

____. 2002 [1996]. *From Cyrus to Alexander: A History of the Persian Empire*. Translated from the French by Peter T. Daniels. Winona Lake, Indiana: Eisenbrauns. This is essentially the same text as the French edition of 1996, *Histoire de l'Empire perse* (Paris: Arthème Fayard, 1996). Supplements are provided in Briant 1997 and 2001.

Briant, Pierre; and Raymond Descat. 1998. Un registre douanier de la satrapie d'Égypte à l'époque achéménide (*TAD* C3,7). In *Le commerce en Égypte ancienne*, edited by Nicolas Grimal and Bernadette Menu. IFAO Bibliothèque d'Étude, 121. Pp. 59–104. Cairo: Institut français d'Archéologie orientale.

Chassinat, Émile. 1932. *Le temple d'Edfou*. vol. 7. Mémoires publiés par les Membres de la Mission archéologique française au Caire, 25. Cairo: Institut français d'Archéologie orientale.

Clay, Albert T. 1904. *Business Documents of Murashû Sons of Nippur Dated in the Reign of Darius II (424–404 B.C.)*. Babylonian Expedition of the University of Pennsylvania, Series A, Cuneiform Texts, vol. 10. Philadelphia: Dept. of Archaeology and Palaeontology of the University of Pennsylvania.

____. 1908. *Legal and Commercial Transactions Dated in the Assyrian, Neo-Babylonian and Persian Periods . . . Chiefly from Nippur*. Babylonian Expedition of the University of Pennsylvania, Series A, Cuneiform Texts, vol. 8, no. 1. Philadelphia: Dept. of Archaeology and Palaeontology of the University of Pennsylvania.

____. 1912. *Business Documents of Murashû Sons of Nippur Dated in the Reign of Darius II*. Pennsylvania. University. University Museum. Publications of the Babylonian Section, vol. 2, no. 1. Philadelphia: University Museum.

Crusius, Paulus. 1578. *Liber de epochis seu aeris temporum et imperiorum omnium facultatum studiosis utilissimus*. Basileae: Per Sebastianum Henricpetri.

Depuydt, Leo. 1995a. The Date of Death of Artaxerxes I. *Welt des Orients* 26: 86–96.

____. 1995b. Regnal Years and Civil Calendar in Achaemenid Egypt. *Journal of Egyptian Archaeology* 81: 151–73.

____. 1995c. Evidence for Accession Dating under the Achaemenids. *Journal of the American Oriental Society* 115: 193–204.

____. 1995d. "More Valuable than All Gold": Ptolemy's Royal Canon and Babylonian Chronology. *Journal of Cuneiform Studies* 47: 97–117.

____. 1996. Egyptian Regnal Dating under Cambyses and the Date of the Persian Conquest. In *Studies in Honor of William Kelly Simpson*, edited by Peter Der Manuelian. Pp. 179–90. Boston: Museum of Fine Arts, Department of Ancient Egyptian, Nubian, and Near Eastern Art.

_____. 1997. The Time of Death of Alexander the Great: 11 June 323 B.C. (-322), ca. 4:00-5:00 PM. *Die Welt des Orients* 28: 117-35.

_____. 2002. The Date of Death of Jesus of Nazareth. *Journal of the American Oriental Society* 122: 466-80.

_____. 2006a. Saite and Persian Egypt, 664-332 BC (Dynasties 26-31, Psammetichus I to Alexander's Conquest of Egypt). In Hornung et al. 2006: 265-83.

_____. 2006b. Foundations of Day-exact Chronology. In Hornung et al. 2006: 458-470.

_____. 2007. Calendars and Years in Ancient Egypt: The Soundness of Egyptian and West Asian Chronology in 1500-500 BC and the Consistency of the Egyptian 365-Day Wandering Year. In Steele 2007: 35-81.

_____. 2008. Ancient Chronology's Alpha and Egyptian Chronology's Debt to Babylon." In Ross 2008: 35-50.

Donbaz, Veysel; and Matthew W. Stolper. 1997. *Istanbul Murašû Texts.* Uitgaven van het Nederlands Historisch-Archaeologisch Instituut te Istanbul, 79. Istanbul: Nederlands Historisch-Archaeologisch Instituut te Istanbul. For an edition of additional tablets from Nippur, see Stolper 2001.

Gauthier, Henri. 1916. *Le livre des rois d'Égypte*, IV: *De la XXVe Dynastie à la fin des Ptolémées.* Mémoires publiés par les Membres de l'Institut français d'Archéologie orientale. Cairo: IFAO.

Glanville, Stephen Ranulph Kingdon. 1939. *Catalogue of Demotic Papyri in the British Museum*, I: *A Theban Archive of the Reign of Ptolemy I Soter.* London: The British Museum.

Goldstine, Herman H. 1973. *New and Full Moons 1001 B.C. to A.D. 1651.* Memoirs of the American Philosophical Society Held at Philadelphia for Promoting Useful Knowledge, 94. Philadelphia: American Philosophical Society.

Gropp, Douglas M. 2001. *Wadi Daliyeh II: The Samaria Papyri from Wadi Daliyeh.* Discoveries in the Judean Desert, 28. Oxford: Clarendon Press.

Grzybek, Erhard. 1990. *Du calendrier macédonien au calendrier ptolémaïque: Problèmes de chronologie hellénistique.* Schweizerische Beiträge zur Altertumswissenschaft, 20. Basel: Friedrich Reinhardt Verlag.

Hölbl, Gustav. 1994. *Geschichte des Ptolemäerreiches: Politik, Ideologie und religiöse Kultur von Alexander dem Großen bis zur römischen Eroberung.* Darmstadt: Wissenschaftliche Buchgesellschaft.

Hornung, Erik; Rolf Krauss; and David A. Warburton (eds.). 2006. *Ancient Egyptian Chronology.* Handbook of Oriental Studies, 83. Leiden and Boston: E.J. Brill.

Hunger, Hermann; including materials by Abraham J. Sachs; with an appendix by John M. Steele. 2001. *Astronomical Diaries and Related Texts from Babylonia*, V: *Lunar and Planetary Texts.* Österreichische Akademie der Wissenschaften, Philosophisch-historische Klasse, 299. Vienna: Verlag der Akademie.

Ideler, Ludwig. 1806. *Historische Untersuchungen über die astronomischen Beobachtungen der Alten.* Berlin: C. Quien.

_____. 1821. Ueber das Todesjahr Alexanders des Großen. *Abhandlungen der Königlichen Akademie der Wissenschaften zu Berlin aus den Jahren 1820-1821.* Pp. 261-88. Berlin: Georg Reimer.

Joannès, Francis. 2006. La Babylonie méridionale: continuité, déclin ou rupture. In: *La transition entre l'empire achéménide et les royaumes hellénistiques*, edited by Pierre Briant and Francis Joannès. Persika, 9. Pp. 101-135. Paris: De Boccard.

Jonsson, Carl Olof. 2004. *The Gentile Times Reconsidered.* Atlanta: Commentary Press.

Jursa, Michael. 1997. Neu- und spätbabylonische Texte aus den Sammlungen der Birmingham Museums und Art Gallery. *Iraq* 59: 97-174.

Kienitz, Friedrich Karl. 1953. *Die politische Geschichte Ägyptens vom 7. bis zum 4. Jahrhundert vor der Zeitwende.* Berlin: Akademie-Verlag.

König, Friedrich Wilhelm. 1972. *Die Persika des Ktesias von Knidos.* Archiv für Orientforschung, Beiheft 18. Graz: Im Selbstverlage des Herausgebers (Ernst Weidner).

Kugler, Franz Xaver. 1900. *Die babylonische Mondrechnung: Zwei Systeme der Chaldäer über den Lauf des Mondes und der Sonne.* Freiburg im Breisgau: Herder'sche Verlagsbuchhandlung.

_____. 1907-24. *Sternkunde und Sterndienst in Babel.* 2 vols. (1 [1907], 2.1 (pp. 1-200) [1909/1910], 2.2.1 (pp. 201-320) [1912], 2.2.2 (pp. 321-630) [1924]) with supplements 1 (1913) and 2 (1914). Münster in Westfalen: Aschendorffsche Verlagsbuchhandlung. A third supplement, by Johann Schaumberger, appeared in 1935.

_____. 1922. *Von Moses bis Paulus: Forschungen zur Geschichte Israels nach biblischen und profangeschichtlichen insbesondere neuen keilinschriftlichen Quellen.* Münster: Aschendorffsche Verlagsbuchhandlung.

Kuhrt, Amélie. 2007. *The Persian Empire: A Corpus of Sources from the Achaemenid Period.* New York: Routledge. I have not seen this.

Lloyd, Alan B. 1988. Manetho and the Thirty-first Dynasty. In *Pyramid Studies and Other Essays Presented to I.E.S. Edwards.* Edited by John Baines, T.G.H. James, Anthony Leahy, and A.F. Shore. EES Occasional Publications, 7. Pp. 154-60. London: The Egypt Exploration Society.

_____. 1994. Egypt, 404-332 B.C. In *The Cambridge Ancient History, Second Edition.* vol. 6. Pp. 337-60, 981-87. Cambridge: University Press.

Maspero, Gaston. 1904. Deux monuments de la princesse Ankhnasnofiribrî. *Annales du Service des Antiquités d'Égypte* 5: 84-90.

McEwan, G.J.P. 1985. The First Seleucid Document from Babylonia. *Journal of Semitic Studies* 30: 169-80.

Meyer, Eduard. 1896. *Die Entstehung des Judentums: Eine historische Untersuchung.* Halle a.S.: Max Niemeyer.

_____. 1899. *Forschungen zur Alten Geschichte*, II: *Zur Geschichte des fünften Jahrhunderts v. Chr.* Halle a.S.: Max Niemeyer.

Mond, Robert; and Oliver H. Myers; with others. 1934. *The Bucheum.* 3 vols. Memoirs of the Egypt Exploration Society, 41. London: The Egypt Exploration Society.

Ni 2668 = tablet Ni(ppur) 2668 published by Donbaz and Stolper (1997: 99–100 [no. 23]).

Oppert, Julius. 1897. Die Schaltmonate bei den Babyloniern und die ägyptisch-chaldäische Ära des Nabonassar. *Zeitschrift der Deutschen Morgenländischen Gesellschaft* 51: 138–65.

Parker, Richard A.; and Waldo H. Dubberstein. 1956. *Babylonian Chronology.* Brown University Studies, 19. Providence: Brown University Press. According to a careful annotation in the Brown University Library copy, the reprint of 1961 George Banta Company of Menasha, Wisc. contains three minor corrections in the tables of dates on pp. 27, 29, and 36. I have not located them.

PBS II.1 = Clay 1912.

PD = Parker and Dubberstein 1956.

Pestman, Pieter Willem. 1967. *Chronologie égyptienne d'après les textes démotiques (332 av. J.-C. - 453 ap. J.-C.).* Papyrologica Lugduno-Batava, 15. Leiden: E.J. Brill.

Pinches, Theodore G.; and Johann Nepomuk Strassmaier (prepared for publication by Abraham J. Sachs with the co-operation of Johann Schaumberger). *Late Babylonian Astronomical and Related Texts.* Brown University Studies, 18. Providence, Rhode Island: Brown University Press.

Porten, Bezalel. 1990. The Calendar of Aramaic Texts from Achaemenid and Ptolemaic Egypt. In *Irano-Judaica*, II: *Studies Relating to Jewish Contacts with Persian Culture throughout the Ages.* Edited by Shaul Shaked and Ammon Netzer. Pp. 13–32. Jerusalem: Makhon Ben-Tsevi.

Porten, Bezalel; and Ada Yardeni. 1986–99. *Textbook of Aramaic Documents from Ancient Egypt.* Newly copied, edited, and translated into Hebrew and English by —. 4 vols. (1986, 1989, 1993, and 1999). Jerusalem: Akademon; distributed by Eisenbrauns, Indiana, U.S.A.

_____. 2008. The Chronology of the Idumean Ostraca in the Decade or so after the Death of Alexander the Great and Its Relevance for Historical Events. In: *Treasures on Camels' Humps: Historical and Literary Studies from the Ancient Near East Presented to Israel Eph'al*, edited by Mordechai Cogan and Dan'el Kahn. Pp. 237–49. Jerusalem: The Hebrew University Magnes Press.

Ross, Micah (ed.). 2008. *From the Banks of the Euphrates: Studies in Honor of Alice Louise Slotsky.* Winona Lake, Indiana: Eisenbrauns.

Sachs, Abraham J.; and Hermann Hunger. 1988. *Astronomical Diaries and Related Texts from Babylonia,* I: *Diaries from 652 B.C. to 262 B.C.* Österreichische Akademie der Wissenschaften, Philosophisch-historische Klasse, 195. Vienna: Verlag der Akademie.

Schrader, Rudolf. 1889. *De Alexandri Magni Vitae Tempore*: *Dissertatio historica.* Bonn (Bonnae): Karl Georg (Typis Caroli Georgi).

Schram, Robert and Gabriele. 1908. *Kalendariographische und chronologische Tafeln.* Leipzig: J.C. Hinrichs'sche Buchhandlung.

Sidersky, David. 1916. *Étude sur la chronologie assyro-babylonienne.* Extrait des Mémoires présentés par divers savants à l'Académie des inscriptions et belles-lettres, 13. Paris: Imprimerie nationale.

Skeat, Theodore Cressy. 1969. *The Reigns of the Ptolemies.* Second edition. Münchener Beiträge zur Papyrusforschung und Antiken Rechtsgeschichte, 39. München: C.H. Beck.

Spiegelberg, Wilhelm. 1902. *Die demotischen Papyrus der Strassburger Bibliothek.* Strassburg i.E.: Verlag von Schlesier & Schweikhardt.

_____. 1907. *Der Papyrus Libbey: Ein ägyptischer Heiratsvertrag.* Schriften der Wissenschaftlichen Gesellschaft in Strassburg, 1. Strassburg: Karl J. Trübner.

Steele, John M. (ed.). 2007. *Calendars and Years: Astronomy and Time in the Ancient Near East.* Oxford: Oxbow Books.

Steele, John M.; and Annette Imhausen (eds.). 2002. *Under One Sky.* Alter Orient und Altes Testament, 297. Münster: Ugarit-Verlag.

Stolper, Matthew W. 1983. The Death of Artaxerxes I. *Archäologische Mitteilungen aus Iran NF* 16: 223–36.

_____. 1994. "Mesopotamia, 482–330 B.C." In: *The Cambridge Ancient History, Second Edition*, VI: *The Fourth Century B.C.* Pp. 234–60. Cambridge: Cambridge University Press.

_____. 1999. Late Achaemenid Babylonian Chronology. *Nouvelles assyriologiques brèves et utilitaires* 1999/6.

_____. 2001. Fifth Century Nippur: Texts of the Murašûs and from Their Surroundings. *Journal of Cuneiform Studies* 53: 83–132.

Swerdlow, Noel (ed.). 1999. *Ancient Astronomy and Celestial Divination.* Cambridge, Mass.: MIT Press.

van der Spek, R.J. 1998. The Chronology of the Wars of Artaxerxes II in the Babylonian Astronomical Diaries. In: *Studies in Persian History: Essays in Memory of David M. Lewis*, edited by Maria Brosius and Amélie Kuhrt. Achaemenid History, 11. Leiden: Nederlands Instituut voor het Nabije Oosten.

von Weiher, Egbert. 1998. *Uruk: Spätbabylonische Texte aus dem Planquadrat U 18. Teil V.* Ausgrabungen in Uruk-Warka: Endberichte, 13. Mainz am Rhein: Verlag Philipp Von Zabern.

Walker, Christopher. 1997. Achaemenid Chronology and the Babylonian Sources. In: *Mesopotamia and Iran in the Persian Period: Conquest and Imperialism*, edited by John Curtis. Pp. 17–25. London: British Museum Press.

Wheatley, Pat. 1998. The Chronology of the Third Diadoch War, 315–311 B.C. *Phoenix* 52: 257–81.

_____. 2002. Antigonus Monophthalmus in Babylonia. *Journal of Near Eastern Studies* 61: 39–47.

Zawadzki, Stefan. 1995-96. The Circumstances of Darius II's Accession in the Light of BM 54557 as against Ctesias' Account. *Jaarbericht "Ex Oriente Lux"* 34: 45–49.

INDICES

The first and last numbers of more than two consecutive pages are connected by an En-dash (–), even when the references are not connected by content.

1. INDEX OF PASSAGES CITED

The referenced pages are those on which the citation is found. But the discussion of the citation may extend to the preceding or following page or pages. Many but by no means all abbreviations are resolved in the section entitled "Abbreviations and References" on pages 81–86. For some abbreviations and for references to the publication of many a source, one will need to consult the publication from which the reference to the source has been taken.

1.1. Aramaic Sources

"C 6" (Porten 1986–99)	9, 17
Idumean Ostrakon	
no. 21	76
no. 22	76
no. 26	70^y, 76
no. 27	70^y, 76
no. 36	76
no. 40	76
no. 43	76
no. 44	76
ISAP	
no. 1245. *See* Idumean Ostrakon no. 27	
no. 1546. *See* Idumean Ostrakon no. 26	
Wadi Daliyeh (Gropp 2001)	41, 69^f

1.2. Bible Passages

Ezra	34
10:15	34
10:16	34
Nehemiah	34
1:1	14, 34
2:1	34
7:73	34
8:2	34
9:1	34
9:1–5	34
9:38	34
Esther	
1: 2,5	14
Daniel	
8: 2	14

1.3. Cuneiform Sources

AION Suppl.
    77 87, lines 19–20   57, 70[z]

AUWE 13
    no. 307   9

Babylonian Chronicle   6, 23

Babylon King List. *See*
    Iraq 16

BaM Beih. II (Uruk King List)
    88   59

BE
    55770   35
    55953   35

BE
    VIII.1
        no. 127   21
    X
        no. 1   21, 28–30
        no. 2   21, 28, 31
        no. 3   21, 30, 31
        no. 4   21, 30
        no. 5   21, 22
        no. 6   21
        no. 109   28

Bertin
    2889   8, 13, 16, 19–21, 28–30

B(ritish) M(useum tablets)
    22022   59, 70[bb], 77
    32234   9
        ´Rev.´ IV´ 4´   24
    32337   6
    32238   25, 53, 58, 70[s, u], 76, 79
        Rev.´ V´ 12´   53
        Rev.´ V´ 12´–13´   79
    32240   69[r]
    32430   69[r]
    32489   69[r]
    33342   21, 29, 30
    34075   26
    34093 + 35758   69[r], 79
    34684 + 34787   13, 16, 22, 27
        Rev.´ I´   27
        Rev.´ I´ 2´   27
        Rev.´ I´ 3´   27
        Rev.´ II´ 1´–3´   27
        Rev.´ II´ 1´–6´   24
    34787. *See* 34684

35024 + 35064 + 35087 + 35618 + 35632 + 45955		69^n
35064. *See* 35024		
35087. *See* 35024		
35531 + 45740		45
35618. *See* 35024		
35632. *See* 35024		
35758. *See* 34093		
36761		69^k
	´Obv.´ 14´–19´	25
	´Obv.´ 15´–18´	3
36910 + 36998 + 37036		19, 27, 31
36998. *See* 36910		
37036. *See* 36910		
40078 + 40105		70^{dd}
40105. *See* 40078		
45740. *See* 35531		
45766		7, 69^q
45955. *See* 35024		
45962		25, 48
48063 + 48069		69^b
48069. *See* 48063		
54557		8, 13, 16, 18–22, 28, 29, 31–33
71537		9, 37, 69^c
	II´ Obv. 1´–5´	24, 37
	II´ Rev. 5–9	37
	III´ Rev. 8–10	24, 25, 39
78603		59, 71^{gg}, 77
78948		56, 76
79012		56, 70^w, 76
87241		45
105211		58

BRM
    2 51   77

CBS (Philadelphia)
    10059   9

CT
    4 29*d*   59, 77
    49 13   56, 70^y, 76
    49 25   77
    49 34   56, 57
    49 50   58

H(arvard) S(emitic) M(useum)
    1893.5.29   41, 69^l

Iraq 16 (Babylon King List)
    plate 53   59, 60

King List of Babylon. *See Iraq* 16

King List of Uruk. *See BaM Beih.* II

Nippur
   2668   21, 28

PBS
   II.1
      no. 1   21, 22

Rm 792 69^r

TBER 88 (AO 26765 [Paris]) 58

Uruk King List. *See BaM*
   Beih. II

VAS (Berlin) VI 186   37

ZA 3 148–49   77

1.4. Demotic Egyptian Sources

Bibliothèque nationale, papyrus
   219   53, 70^s, 77

Libbey, papyrus   44

Loeb, papyrus
   27   53, 55, 70^y, 77

Louvre, papyri
   2427   55, 71^{ff}, 77
   2430   44
   2439   44
   2440   55, 71^{ff}, 77

Strassburg, papyrus
   1   44, 69^p

1.5. Greek Sources

Aelian
   Varia Historia
      XIII 3   9

Anecdota Graeca (Bekker)
   I 23   50

Aristoboulos   49, 50

Arrian
   Anabasis   49
      III 1,1   43

Canon, Ptolemy's Royal   2, 8, 35, 41,
                                   43, 46, 48,
                                   55, 61, 63,
                                   $69^{e,\,g,\,j,\,o}$

Demetrios of Phaleron	14	
Diodoros		
World History	16, 17, 49, 75	
II 32	13	
XI 11,4	54	
XI 11,5	54	
XII 64	15	
XII 64,1–65,1	16	
XII 71,1	14	
XIV 46,6	14	
XV 93,1	26	
XVII 5,4	41, 69[f]	
XVII 48,7	43	
XIX 11	54	
XIX 55–56,1	57	
Eusebios	49	
Kallisthenes, pseudo-	44, 47, 48	
Ktesias		
Persika (König 1972)	13, 14, 16, 19, 31, 32, 35	
§1	35	
§12	14	
§43	14	
§44	14	
§46	14	
§47	14	
§48	14	
§49	14	
§§43–49	13	
§56	14, 35	
§60	35	
Photios,		
transmitting Ktesias	13, 31, 35	
Plutarch		
Life of Alexander		
16	50	
75,6	50	
76,9	50	
Life of Camillus		
19,5	55	
Thucydides		
History	19	
IV 50	15, 16, 28	
IV 52	16, 28	
VIII 58	32	

1.6. Hieroglyphic Egyptian Sources

Ankhnesneferibre, Stela of   10

Buchis stela   44

Edfu ed. Chassinat
    1932: 9,3–4   10

Luxor graffito   44

1.7. Latin Sources

Cicero
    De oratore
        II 58   49

Justinus
    abridger of Trogus
        XII 16,1   49

Trogus, Pompeius
    Historiae Philippicae   49

2. INDEX OF MODERN AUTHORS CITED

Please note that:
(1) as an author's name may occur more than once on a referenced page, scanning the whole page may be necessary to establish whether it does.
(2) authors are referenced only when a specific opinion they hold on a certain matter is explicitly cited or discussed.

Beloch, Karl Julius
44
Boiy, Tom
45, 56–59, 63
Briant, Pierre
14, 18, 26, 31, 33, 37, 61, 62

Champollion-Figeac, Jacques-Joseph
49
Clay, Albert
18, 28
Crusius, Paul
48

Des-Vignoles, Alphonse
48
Dodwell, Henry
48

Fréret, Nicolas
48

Gauthier, Henri
44
Grzybek, Erhard
43, 44

Hunger, Hermann
9, 27, 28

Ideler, Ludwig
47–50

Joannès, Francis
8

Kugler, Franz Xaver
17–22, 28–30, 34, 60

McEwan, G.J.P
59
Meyer, Eduard
15, 17, 18, 33, 34, 44

Parker, Richard A.
48, 77
Petavius, Dionysius (Denys Petau)
47, 48

Sachs, Abraham
27
Saint-Martin, Antoine Jean
48
Sainte-Croix, Guillaume-Emmanouel
-Joseph
48
Scaliger, Joseph Justus
47, 48
Schrader, Rudolf
47, 48
Sidersky, David
7, 63
Skeat, Theodore Cressy
44
Steele, John
27
Stolper, Matthew
9

Ussher, James
48

Walker, Christopher
9, 11, 23, 28, 37

Zawadzki, Stefan
14, 18

3. INDEX OF SUBJECTS TREATED

A term may occur more than once on a page to which reference is made. Scanning the entire page is hence desirable to establish whether it does. This brief index is not designed to reference every subject comprehensively. Its limited aim is to locate a select number of subjects or discussions of subjects falling outside this work's main argument. Thus, subjects mentioned in the titles of sections are typically not included. Nor are frequently mentioned subjects likely to be found in this index. A couple of Babylonian and Greek terms are listed at the end.

Accession year (Babylonian MU.SAG), period lasting from a Babylonian king's accession to the first New Year's Day when his Year 1 begins, 8, 9, 17, 18, 23, 25, 30, 34, 35, 41, 44, 45, 53, 59, 77
"Achaemenid": definition of, 3–4
Achaemenid dynasty: origin of, 3
Achaemenid Persia: pivotal place of, in world history, 3–4
Alexander the Great: as one of five Pharaohs whose date of death is known to the exact day, 10, 12
Alogune (Alogyne), a wife of Artaxerxes I and mother of Sekyndianos, 14
Apollodoros of Athens: as ancient student of chronology, 49
Aramaic papyri from Egypt: role of, in securing the veracity of earliest day-exact dating, 4
Arr(h)idaios, Philip: as one of five Pharaohs whose date of death is known to the exact day, 10–12

Babylonian astronomy
—empirical foundations of, 5
—as longest research project in history, 6
—prescientific character of, 4, 5
Bagoas, courtier who had both Artaxerxes III and his son Arses murdered, 39, 41
Beloch, Karl Julius: as student of chronology, 44

Cambyses: transition of reign involving, 1, 2
Crusius, Paul: as pioneer of "BC" chronology, 48
Cyrus, ruler of Babylon: transition of reign involving, 1, 2, 23
Cyrus, son of Darius II, 35

Damaspia, mother of Xerxes II, 14
Darius I: transition of reign involving, 1, 2
Day: beginning of, 54
Day-exact dating: beginning of, in world history, 4
Deaths of Pharaohs of which the date is known to the exact day, 9–12

Eclipse: as reference-point for dating a historical event, 16, 23, 26–28, 37
Epping, Julius: as decipherer of Babylonian astronomy, 7
Eratosthenes of Cyrene: as ancient student of chronology, 49
Ezra: as Artaxerxes I's emissary to Jerusalem, 33

Gaza: siege of, by Alexander the Great, 43

Ḥašba, a town near Nippur: as origin of a tablet dating to Artaxerxes I after his death, 28, 29
Hipparchus of Rhodes, discoverer of trigonometry, 4

Ideler, Ludwig: as pioneer of "BC" chronology, 48; as student of the date of Alexander's death, 15, 47–50

Khababash, Pharaoh, 44
Ktesias of Knidos: reliability of, as historian, 13, 14
Kugler, Franz Xaver: as decipherer of Babylonian astronomy, 7; as student of chronology, 14, 17, 18, 19

Macedonian lunar calendar, 50, 55
Meyer, Eduard: interpretation by, of Artaxerxes I's "Year 41," 17, 18

Nabopolassar: transitions of reign involving, 23
Naqš i-Rustam, burial place of Achaemenid kings, 14
Nebuchadrezzar: transition of reign involving, 23
Nehemiah: as Artaxerxes I's emissary to Jerusalem, 33

Ochos: as name of Darius II, 14, 24; as name of Artaxerxes III, 24–26, 31, 37, 39
Olympias, mother of Philip Arridaios, 54

Olympic games: as a reference-point for dating a historical event, 16, 17

Philip Arridaios. *See* Arr(h)idaios
Postdating, 78
Predating, 78
Psammetich II: as one of five Pharaohs whose date of death is known to the exact day, 10, 12
Ptolemy I, 56, 57
Ptolemy VIII Euergetes II: as one of five Pharaohs whose date of death is known to the exact day, 10, 12

Roxane, wife of Alexander the Great and mother of Alexander IV, 56

Saros, Solar, 46, 55, 58, 60, $69^{m,\,q}$, 70^{ee}, 78
Saros Canon, Lunar, 7, 55, 58, 60, $69^{m,\,q}$, $70^{t,\,x,\,ee}$
Schrader, Rudolf: as student of the chronology of Alexander the Great, 47, 48
Sekyndianos (Sekundianos), ephemeral Achaemenid ruler (423 B.C.E.), 14, 19, 20, 31, 32, 61
Seleucid era, 60
Seleukos, general and later king Seleukos I, 56–59

Sidersky, David: as early student and epitomizer of Babylonian astronomy, 7, 63
Sogdianos. *See* Sekyndianos
Sparta: treaty of, with Persia, 32, 33
Strassmaier, Johann: as decipherer of Babylonian astronomy, 7

Thucydides: reliability of, as historian, 16
Timaios of Tauromenium: as ancient student of chronology, 49
Transitions of reign of Achaemenid kings mentioned in Babylonian astronomical texts, 24–26

Xerxes I: as one of five Pharaohs whose date of death is known to the exact day, 10–12
Xerxes II, ephemeral Achaemenid ruler (423 B.C.E.), 14, 19, 31

Babylonian

EDIN "open country," 27
IDI "was seen," 27
MU.SAG "accession year," 8, 23

Greek

δείλη "late afternoon," 50, 51